chocolate

100 everyday recipes

First published in 2011
LOVE FOOD is an imprint of Parragon Books Ltd

Parragon
Queen Street House
4 Queen Street
Bath BA1 1HE, UK

ISBN: 978-1-4454-4287-7

Printed in China

Produced by Ivy Contract
Cover photography by Mike Cooper
Cover image home economy and food styling by Lincoln Jefferson

Notes for the Reader

This book uses imperial, metric, and US cup measurements. Follow the same units of measurement throughout; do not mix imperial and metric. All spoon measurements are level: teaspoons are assumed to be 5 ml, and tablespoons are assumed to be 15 ml. Unless otherwise stated, milk is assumed to be whole, eggs and individual vegetables, such as potatoes, are medium, and pepper is freshly ground black pepper.

The times given are an approximate guide only. Preparation times differ according to the techniques used by different people and the cooking times may also vary from those given as a result of the type of oven used. Optional ingredients, variations, or serving suggestions have not been included in the calculations.

Recipes using raw or very lightly cooked eggs should be avoided by infants, the elderly, pregnant women, convalescents, and anyone with a chronic condition. Pregnant and breast-feeding women are advised to avoid eating peanuts and peanut products. People with nut allergies should be aware that some of the prepared ingredients used in the recipes in this book may contain nuts. Always check the package before use.

Vegetarians should be aware that some of the prepared ingredients used in the recipes in this book may contain animal products. Always check the package before use.

Picture acknowledgments
The publisher would like to thank the following for permission to reproduce copyright material
Front cover: Chocolate pudding © Dennis Gottlieb/Getty Images

chocolate

introduction

The very word "chocolate" almost has a magic about it and those who love it will agree unanimously that the taste is quite definitely magical.

The remarkable story of chocolate dates back to the 7th century, when the cocoa tree, Theobroma cacao, was cultivated by the Maya of Central America. This ancient civilization established a flourishing trade, even using the cocoa bean as currency. The explorer Christopher Columbus took the cocoa bean to Spain in 1502, and Hernán Cortés, who conquered Mexico for Spain, soon afterward got an idea of what to do with this curious object when the Aztec Emperor Montezuma introduced him to xocotlatl, a drink made of crushed, roasted cocoa beans and cold water. This bitter-tasting brew soon evolved into something more pleasant when it was served hot with a flavoring of vanilla, spices, honey, and sugar.

By the late 17th century, Europe and beyond had fallen under the spell of the "hot chocolate" drink, but it is a 19th-century Dutch chemist, Coenraad Van Houten, whom we have to thank for chocolate that we can eat. This veritable hero invented a method of producing pure cocoa butter and a hard "cake" that could be milled to produce cocoa "powder" for flavoring. Within a very short time, the chocolate industry was founded, going from strength to strength as different countries began to produce smooth, melt-in-the-mouth chocolate bars.

Today, to our delight, there is no end to the creative ways in which chocolate is used in cooking. Hot desserts, cakes, cookies, chilled desserts, ice creams—they all seem to have a little extra appeal when they include chocolate.

If you are one of the world's many chocoholics, you'll love this book. Just dip in and be indulgent!

favorite desserts

toffee chocolate puff tarts

ingredients

serves 12

13 oz/375 g prepared puff pastry
5 oz/140 g semisweet chocolate,
    broken into pieces
1¼ cups heavy cream
¼ cup superfine sugar
4 egg yolks
¼ cup store-bought toffee sauce
unsweetened cocoa, for dusting
whipped cream, to serve

method

1 Line the bottoms of a 12-hole nonstick muffin pan with disks of wax paper.

2 Cut out twelve 2-inch/5-cm circles from the edge of the pie dough and cut the remainder into 12 strips. Roll the strips to half their thickness and line the sides of each hole in the pan with one strip. Put a disk of pie dough at the bottom, and press well together to seal and make a tart shell. Prick the bottoms and chill in the refrigerator for 30 minutes.

3 While the pie dough is chilling, melt the chocolate in a heatproof bowl set over a saucepan of gently simmering water. Remove the bowl from the heat, cool slightly, then stir in the cream. Beat the sugar and egg yolks together and mix well with the melted chocolate.

4 Remove the muffin pan from the refrigerator and put a teaspoonful of toffee sauce into each tart shell. Divide the chocolate mixture among the tarts and bake in a preheated oven, 400°F/200°C, for 20–25 minutes, turning the tray around halfway through the cooking, until just set.

5 Remove from the oven and cool the tarts in the muffin pan then remove carefully, leaving behind the wax paper. Dust the tarts with unsweetened cocoa and serve with whipped cream.

cream puffs with chocolate sauce

ingredients

serves 4

choux pastry

generous ¼ cup butter,
    plus extra for greasing
scant 1 cup water
¾ cup all-purpose flour
3 eggs, beaten

cream filling

1¼ cups heavy cream
3 tbsp superfine sugar
1 tsp vanilla extract

chocolate sauce

4½ oz/125 g semisweet chocolate,
    broken into small pieces
3 tbsp butter
⅓ cup water
2 tbsp cognac

method

1 Lightly grease a large cookie sheet. To make the choux pastry, place the butter and water in a saucepan and bring to a boil. Meanwhile, sift the flour into a bowl. Turn off the heat and beat in the flour until smooth. Cool for 5 minutes. Beat in enough of the beaten egg to give the mixture a soft, dropping consistency.

2 Transfer to a pastry bag fitted with a ½-inch/1-cm plain tip. Pipe small balls onto the prepared cookie sheet. Bake in a preheated oven, 400°F/200°C, for 25 minutes.

3 Remove from the oven. Pierce each ball with a skewer to let the steam escape.

4 To make the filling, whip the cream, sugar, and vanilla extract together. Cut the balls across the middle, then fill with the cream mixture.

5 To make the sauce, gently melt the chocolate, butter, and water together in a small saucepan, stirring constantly, until smooth. Stir in the cognac.

6 Pile the cream puffs into individual serving dishes, pour over the sauce, and serve.

chocolate cherry clafoutis

ingredients

serves 6–8

butter, for greasing
1 lb/450 g black cherries,
  pitted
2 tbsp granulated sugar
3 eggs
generous ¼ cup superfine sugar
scant ½ cup self-rising flour
2 tbsp unsweetened cocoa
¾ cup heavy cream
1¼ cups milk
2 tbsp kirsch (optional)
lightly whipped cream,
  to serve

method

1 Lightly grease a 9-inch/23-cm square ovenproof dish. Arrange the cherries in the prepared dish, sprinkle with the granulated sugar, and set aside.

2 Put the eggs and superfine sugar in a bowl and whip together until light and frothy. Sift the flour and cocoa into a separate bowl and add, all at once, to the egg mixture. Beat in thoroughly, then whip in the cream followed by the milk and kirsch, if using. Pour the batter over the cherries.

3 Bake in a preheated oven, 375°F/190°C, for 50–60 minutes, until slightly risen and set in the center.

4 Serve warm with cream.

chocolate nut strudel

ingredients

serves 6

generous 1¼ cups mixed
    chopped nuts
4 oz/115 g semisweet
    chocolate, chopped
4 oz/115 g milk chocolate,
    chopped
4 oz/115 g white chocolate,
    chopped
7 oz/200 g filo dough,
    thawed if frozen
scant ¾ cup butter, plus extra
    for greasing
3 tbsp dark corn syrup

method

1 Lightly grease a baking sheet.

2 Set aside 1 tablespoon of the nuts. Place the remaining
   nuts in a bowl and mix together with the three types
   of chocolate.

3 Place a sheet of filo dough on a clean dish towel. Melt
   the butter and brush the sheet of filo with the butter,
   drizzle with a little corn syrup, and sprinkle with a little
   of the nut-and-chocolate mixture. Repeat the layers
   until you have used up all the filo dough, butter, nuts,
   and chocolate and most of the corn syrup.

4 Use the dish towel to help you carefully roll up the
   strudel and place on the baking sheet, drizzle with a
   little more corn syrup, and sprinkle with the reserved
   nuts. Bake in a preheated oven, 375°F/190°C, for
   20–25 minutes. If the nuts start to brown too much,
   cover the strudel with a sheet of foil. Serve warm.

chocolate & meringue dessert

ingredients

serves 4

1¾oz/50 g semisweet chocolate
2 cups chocolate-flavored milk
1¾ cups fresh white or whole
    wheat breadcrumbs
generous ½ cup superfine sugar
2 eggs, separated
4 oz/100 g cherry jelly

method

1 Break the chocolate into small pieces and place in a saucepan with the chocolate-flavored milk. Heat gently, stirring, until the chocolate melts. Bring almost to a boil, then remove the pan from the heat.

2 Place the breadcrumbs in a large mixing bowl with 5 teaspoons of the superfine sugar. Pour over the chocolate milk and mix well. Beat in the egg yolks.

3 Spoon into a five-cup pie dish and bake in a preheated oven, 350°F/180°C, for 25–30 minutes, or until set and firm to the touch.

4 Whip the egg whites in a large greasefree bowl until soft peaks form. Gradually whip in the remaining superfine sugar and whip until you have a glossy, thick meringue.

5 Spread the cherry jelly over the surface of the chocolate mixture and pile the meringue on top. Return the dessert to the oven for about 15 minutes, or until the meringue is crisp and golden. Serve.

chocolate apple lattice tart

ingredients

serves 6

pie dough

scant 1½ cups all-purpose flour,
plus extra for dusting
2 tbsp unsweetened cocoa
3 tbsp superfine sugar
scant ½ cup unsalted butter, diced,
plus extra for greasing
1–2 egg yolks, beaten

filling

1 cup heavy cream
2 eggs, beaten
1 tsp ground cinnamon
4 oz/115 g semisweet
chocolate, grated
4 apples, peeled, sliced, and
brushed with lemon juice
3 tbsp raw brown sugar

method

1 To make the pie dough, sift the flour and cocoa into
a bowl. Add the superfine sugar, rub in the butter, and
mix well. Stir in enough egg yolk to form a dough.
Form into a ball, wrap in foil, and chill for 45 minutes.

2 Grease an 8-inch/20-cm round loose-bottom tart pan.
Roll out the dough on a lightly floured work surface
and use three-quarters of it to line the pan.

3 For the filling, beat together the cream, eggs (reserving
a little for glazing), cinnamon, and chocolate in a bowl.
Stir in the apples. Spoon into the pastry shell, then
sprinkle over the raw sugar.

4 Roll out the remaining dough and cut into long,
thin strips, then arrange over the tart to form a lattice
pattern. Brush the pastry strips with the reserved
beaten egg, then bake in a preheated oven, 350°F/
180°C, for 40–45 minutes.

5 Remove the tart from the oven and let cool to room
temperature. Serve.

fine chocolate tart

ingredients

serves 6

pie dough

generous 1 cup all-purpose flour
2 tsp unsweetened cocoa
2 tsp confectioners' sugar
pinch of salt
¼ cup cold butter, cut into pieces,
   plus extra for greasing
1 egg yolk
ice-cold water

ganache filling

7 oz/200 g semisweet chocolate
   with 70% cocoa solids
2 tbsp unsalted butter,
   softened
1 generous cup heavy cream
1 tsp dark rum (optional)
chocolate curls, to serve

method

1 Lightly grease a 9-inch/23-cm loose-bottom fluted tart pan. Sift the flour, cocoa, confectioners' sugar, and salt into a food processor, add the butter, and process until the mixture resembles fine breadcrumbs. Tip the mixture into a large bowl, add the egg yolk, and just enough ice-cold water to bring the dough together. Turn out onto a counter dusted with more flour and cocoa and roll out the dough 3¼ inches/8 cm larger than the pan. Carefully lift the dough into the pan and press to fit. Roll the rolling pin over the pan to neaten the edges and trim the excess dough. Fit a piece of parchment paper into the tart shell, fill with dried beans, and let chill in the refrigerator for 30 minutes.

2 Remove the pastry shell from the refrigerator and bake in a preheated oven, 375°F/190°C, for 15 minutes, then remove the beans and paper and bake for an additional 5–10 minutes.

3 To make the ganache filling, chop the chocolate and put in a bowl with the softened butter. Bring the cream to a boil, then pour onto the chocolate, stirring well. Add the rum (if using) and continue stirring to make sure the chocolate is melted completely. Pour into the pastry shell and let chill in the refrigerator for 3 hours. Serve decorated with chocolate curls.

white chocolate & cardamom tart

ingredients

serves 6

pie dough

generous 1 cup all-purpose flour

pinch of salt

generous ¼ cup cold butter,
    cut into pieces

ice-cold water

filling

seeds of 8 cardamom pods,
    crushed to a powder

12 oz/350 g white chocolate,
    chopped into small pieces

2 pieces fine leaf gelatin

cold water

scant 2 cups whipping cream

unsweetened cocoa, for dusting

white chocolate curls, to decorate

method

1 Lightly grease a 9-inch/23-cm loose-bottom fluted tart pan. Sift the flour and salt into a food processor, add the butter, and process until the mixture resembles fine breadcrumbs. Tip into a large bowl and add just enough ice-cold water to bring the dough together. Turn out onto a lightly floured counter and roll out the dough 3¼ inches/8 cm larger than the pan. Carefully lift the dough into the pan and press to fit. Trim the excess dough. Fit a piece of parchment paper into the tart shell, fill with dried beans and let chill in the refrigerator for 30 minutes.

2 Remove the pastry tart from the refrigerator and bake for 15 minutes in a preheated oven, 375°F/190°C. Remove the beans and paper from the tart shell and bake for an additional 10 minutes. Let cool completely.

3 Put the crushed cardamom in a large bowl with the chocolate. Soak the gelatin in a little cold water in a small heat-proof bowl for 5 minutes, then stir over a pan of simmering water until dissolved. Heat the cream until just boiling, then pour over the chocolate, using a whisk to stir until the chocolate has melted, and add the gelatin. Let cool and pour into the tart shell, then let chill in the refrigerator for at least 3 hours. Dust with cocoa and top with chocolate curls.

chocolate fudge tart

ingredients

serves 6–8

12 oz/350 g ready-made
    unsweetened pie dough
flour, for sprinkling
confectioners' sugar, for dusting

filling

5 oz/140 g semisweet chocolate,
    finely chopped
¾ cup butter, diced
1¼ cups golden granulated sugar
¾ cup all-purpose flour
½ tsp vanilla extract
6 eggs, beaten

to decorate

⅔ cup whipped cream
ground cinnamon

method

1 Roll out the pie dough on a lightly floured counter and
   use to line an 8-inch/20-cm deep loose-bottom tart
   pan. Prick the dough base lightly with a fork, then line
   with foil and fill with dried beans. Bake in a preheated
   oven, 400°F/200°C, for 12–15 minutes, or until the
   dough no longer looks raw. Remove the beans and
   foil and bake for an additional 10 minutes, or until the
   dough is firm to the touch. Let cool. Reduce the oven
   temperature to 350°F/180°C.

2 To make the filling, place the chocolate and butter
   in a heatproof bowl and set over a pan of gently
   simmering water until melted. Stir until smooth, then
   remove from the heat and let cool. Place the sugar,
   flour, vanilla extract, and eggs in a separate bowl and
   whisk until well blended. Stir in the butter and
   chocolate mixture.

3 Pour the filling into the pastry shell and bake in the
   oven for 50 minutes, or until the filling is just set.
   Transfer to a wire rack to cool completely. Dust with
   confectioners' sugar before serving with whipped
   cream sprinkled lightly with cinnamon.

chocolate chiffon pie

ingredients

serves 8

nut base
scant 2 cups shelled Brazil nuts
generous ¼ cup granulated sugar
4 tsp melted butter

filling
1 cup milk
2 tsp powdered gelatin
generous ½ cup superfine sugar
2 eggs, separated
8 oz/225 g semisweet chocolate,
    roughly chopped
1 tsp vanilla extract
⅔ cup heavy cream
2 tbsp chopped Brazil nuts,
    to decorate

method

1 Process the whole Brazil nuts in a food processor until finely ground. Add the granulated sugar and melted butter and process briefly to combine. Tip the mixture into a 9-inch/23-cm round tart pan and press it onto the base and side with a spoon. Bake in a preheated oven, 400°F/200°C, for 8–10 minutes, or until light golden brown. Set aside to cool.

2 Pour the milk into a heatproof bowl and sprinkle the gelatin over the surface. Let it soften for 2 minutes, then set over a pan of gently simmering water. Stir in half of the superfine sugar, both the egg yolks, and the chocolate. Stir constantly over low heat for 4–5 minutes until the gelatin has dissolved and the chocolate has melted. Remove from the heat and beat until smooth. Stir in the vanilla extract, cover and let chill in the refrigerator for 45–60 minutes until starting to set.

3 Whip the cream until it is stiff, then fold all but 3 tablespoons into the chocolate mixture. Whip the egg whites in a separate, clean, greasefree bowl until soft peaks form. Add 2 teaspoons of the remaining sugar and whisk until stiff peaks form. Fold in the rest of the sugar, then the egg whites into the chocolate mixture. Pour into the pastry shell and let chill in the refrigerator for 3 hours. Decorate the pie with the whipped cream and the chopped nuts before serving.

pecan & chocolate pie

ingredients

serves 6–8

pie dough

generous 1 cup all-purpose flour,
    plus extra for dusting
scant ½ cup butter, diced
1 tbsp golden superfine sugar
1 egg yolk, beaten with
    1 tbsp water

filling

¼ cup butter
3 tbsp unsweetened cocoa
1 cup corn syrup
3 eggs
scant ½ cup dark brown sugar
¾ cup shelled pecans, chopped

to serve

whipped cream
ground cinnamon, for dusting

method

1 To make the pie dough, sift the flour into a large bowl.
Rub in the butter until the mixture resembles fine
breadcrumbs, then stir in the superfine sugar. Stir in the
beaten egg yolk. Knead lightly to form a firm dough,
cover with plastic wrap, and let chill in the refrigerator
for 1½ hours. Roll out the chilled dough on a lightly
floured counter and use it to line an 8-inch/20-cm
tart pan.

2 To make the filling, place the butter in a small,
heavy-bottom pan and heat gently until melted. Sift
in the cocoa and stir in the syrup. Place the eggs and
sugar in a large bowl and beat together. Add the syrup
mixture and the chopped pecans and stir. Pour the
mixture into the prepared pastry shell.

3 Place the pie on a preheated cookie sheet and bake in
a preheated oven, 375°F/190°C, for 35–40 minutes, or
until the filling is just set. Let cool slightly and serve
warm with a spoonful of whipped cream, dusted with
ground cinnamon.

mississippi mud pie

ingredients

serves 8

pie dough
generous 1½ cups all-purpose
    flour, plus extra for dusting
2 tbsp unsweetened cocoa
scant ¾ cup butter
2 tbsp superfine sugar
1–2 tbsp cold water

filling
¾ cup butter
scant 1¾ cups brown sugar
4 eggs, lightly beaten
1 oz/25 g unsweetened
    cocoa, sifted
5½ oz/150 g semisweet
    chocolate
1¼ cups light cream
1 tsp chocolate extract

to decorate
scant 2 cups heavy cream,
    whipped
chocolate flakes and curls

method

1 To make the pie dough, sift the flour and cocoa into a mixing bowl. Rub in the butter with the fingertips until the mixture resembles fine breadcrumbs. Stir in the sugar and enough cold water to mix to a soft dough. Wrap the dough in foil or plastic wrap and let chill in the refrigerator for 15 minutes.

2 Roll out the dough on a lightly floured counter and use to line a 9-inch/23-cm loose-bottom tart pan or ceramic pie dish. Line with parchment paper and fill with dried beans. Bake in a preheated oven, 375°F/190°C, for 15 minutes. Remove from the oven and take out the paper and beans. Bake the pastry shell for an additional 10 minutes.

3 To make the filling, beat the butter and sugar together in a bowl and gradually beat in the eggs with the cocoa. Melt the chocolate and beat it into the mixture with the light cream and the chocolate extract.

4 Reduce the oven temperature to 325°F/160°C. Pour the mixture into the pastry shell and bake for 45 minutes, or until the filling has set gently.

5 Let the mud pie cool completely, then transfer it to a serving plate, if you like. Cover with the whipped cream Decorate the pie with chocolate flakes and curls and then let chill in the refrigerator until ready to serve.

chocolate crumble pie

ingredients

serves 8

pie dough
scant 1½ cups all-purpose flour
1 tsp baking powder
½ cup unsalted butter, cut into
    small pieces
scant ¼ cup superfine sugar
1 egg yolk
1–2 tsp cold water

filling
⅔ cup heavy cream
⅔ cup milk
8 oz/225 g semisweet chocolate,
    chopped
2 eggs

crumble topping
generous ½ cup brown sugar
¾ cup toasted pecans
4 oz/115 g semisweet chocolate
3 oz/85 g amaretti cookies
1 tsp unsweetened cocoa

method

1 To make the pie dough, sift the flour and baking powder into a large bowl, rub in the butter, and stir in the sugar, then add the egg yolk and a little water to bring the dough together. Turn the dough out, and knead briefly. Wrap the dough in foil or plastic wrap and let chill in the refrigerator for 30 minutes.

2 Roll out the pie dough and use to line a 9-inch/23-cm loose-bottom tart pan. Prick the pastry shell with a fork. Line with parchment paper and fill with dried beans. Bake in a preheated oven, 375°F/190°C, for 15 minutes. Remove from the oven and take out the paper and beans. Reduce the oven temperature to 350°F/180°C.

3 Bring the cream and milk to a boil in a pan, remove from the heat, and add the chocolate. Stir until melted and smooth. Beat the eggs and add to the chocolate mixture, mix thoroughly and pour into the shell. Bake for 15 minutes, remove the pie from the oven, and let rest for 1 hour.

4 When you are ready to serve the pie, place all the topping ingredients in the food processor and pulse to create a chunky crumble topping. Sprinkle over the pie and serve.

chocolate blueberry pies

ingredients

serves 10

pie dough
scant 1½ cups all-purpose flour
½ cup unsweetened cocoa
generous ¼ cup superfine sugar
pinch of salt
generous ½ cup butter, cut into
    small pieces
1 egg yolk
1–2 tbsp cold water

sauce
1⅛ cups blueberries
2 tbsp crème de cassis
scant ⅛ cup confectioners' sugar,
    sifted

filling
5 oz/140 g semisweet chocolate,
    broken into pieces
1 cup heavy cream
⅔ cup sour cream

method

1 To make the pie dough, place the flour, cocoa, sugar, and salt in a large bowl and rub in the butter until the mixture resembles breadcrumbs. Add the egg yolk and a little water to form a dough. Wrap the dough in foil and let chill in the refrigerator for 30 minutes.

2 Remove the pie dough from the refrigerator and roll out. Use to line 10 x 4-inch/10-cm tart pans. Freeze for 30 minutes. Bake in a preheated oven, 350°F/180°C, for 15–20 minutes. Let cool.

3 To make the sauce, place the blueberries, cassis, and the confectioners' sugar in a pan and warm through so that the berries become shiny but do not burst. Set aside to cool.

4 To make the filling, melt the chocolate in a heatproof bowl set over a pan of simmering water, then let cool slightly. Whip the cream until stiff and fold in the sour cream and chocolate.

5 Remove the pastry shells to serving plates and divide the chocolate filling between them, smoothing the surface with a spatula, then top with the blueberries. Serve with the sauce.

chocolate ginger puddings

ingredients

serves 4

generous ⅓ cup soft margarine
¾ cup self-rising flour, sifted
½ cup superfine sugar
2 eggs
¼ cup unsweetened cocoa, sifted
1 oz/25 g semisweet chocolate
1¼ oz/50 g preserved ginger, plus
    extra to garnish
raw brown sugar, for topping

chocolate sauce

2 egg yolks
1 tbsp superfine sugar, plus
    extra for dusting
1 tbsp cornstarch
1¼ cups milk
3½ oz/100 g semisweet chocolate,
    broken into pieces

method

1 Lightly grease 4 small individual ovenproof bowls.

2 Place the margarine, flour, sugar, eggs, and cocoa in a mixing bowl and beat until well combined and smooth. Chop the chocolate and preserved ginger and stir into the mixture, ensuring they are well combined.

3 Divide the cake mixture between the prepared bowls and smooth the tops. Cover the bowls with disks of baking parchment and cover with a pleated sheet of foil. Cook the mini chocolate gingers in a steamer for 45 minutes, until the sponges are cooked and springy to the touch.

4 Meanwhile, make the sauce. Beat the egg yolks, sugar, and cornstarch together to form a smooth paste. Heat the milk until boiling and pour over the egg mixture. Return to the pan and cook over very low heat, stirring until thick. Remove from the heat and beat in the chocolate. Stir until the chocolate melts.

5 Lift the chocolate gingers from the steamer, run a knife around the edge of the bowls, and carefully turn out onto serving plates. Dust each chocolate ginger with sugar and drizzle chocolate sauce over the top. Decorate with preserved ginger. Serve the remaining chocolate sauce separately.

sticky chocolate puddings

ingredients

serves 6

generous ½ cup butter, softened
¾ cup brown sugar
3 eggs, beaten
pinch of salt
¼ cup unsweetened cocoa
scant 1 cup self-rising flour
1 oz/25 g semisweet chocolate,
  finely chopped
2¾ oz/75 g white chocolate,
  finely chopped

sauce

⅔ cup heavy cream
scant ½ cup brown sugar
2 tbsp butter

method

1 Lightly grease six individual ¾-cup ovenproof individual dessert molds.

2 Cream the butter and sugar together in a bowl until pale and fluffy. Beat in the eggs a little at a time, beating well after each addition. Sift the salt, cocoa, and flour into the creamed mixture, and fold. Stir in the chopped chocolate until evenly combined throughout

3 Divide the mixture between the prepared molds. Lightly grease six squares of foil and use them to cover the tops of the molds, pressing around the edges to seal. Place the molds in a roasting pan and pour in boiling water to come halfway up the sides of the molds. Bake in a preheated oven, 350°F/180°C, for 50 minutes, or until a skewer inserted into the center of the sponges comes out clean. Remove the molds from the roasting pan and set aside.

4 To make the sauce, put the cream, sugar, and butter into a pan and bring to a boil over a gentle heat. Simmer gently until the sugar has completely dissolved, then transfer to a warm pitcher.

5 To serve, run a knife around the edge of each sponge, then turn out onto serving plates. Serve immediately with the pitcher of sauce for pouring over.

individual chocolate puddings

ingredients

serves 4

pudding

½ cup superfine sugar

3 eggs

½ cup all-purpose flour

½ cup unsweetened cocoa

scant ½ cup unsalted butter,
    melted, plus extra for greasing

3½ oz/100 g semisweet
    chocolate, melted

chocolate sauce

2 tbsp unsalted butter

3½ oz/100 g semisweet chocolate

generous ¼ cup water

1 tbsp superfine sugar

1 tbsp coffee-flavored liqueur,
    such as Kahlúa

coffee beans, to decorate

method

1 Grease 4 small heatproof bowls with butter.

2 To make the desserts, put the sugar and eggs into a
heatproof bowl and place over a pan of simmering
water. Whisk for about 10 minutes, until frothy. Remove
the bowl from the heat and fold in the flour and
cocoa. Fold in the butter, then the chocolate. Mix well.

3 Spoon the mixture into the bowls and cover with
waxed paper. Top with foil and secure with string.
Place in a large pan filled with enough simmering
water to reach halfway up the sides of the bowls.
Steam for about 40 minutes, or until cooked through.

4 About 2–3 minutes before the end of the cooking
time, make the sauce. Put the butter, chocolate,
water, and sugar into a small pan and warm over a low
heat, stirring constantly, until melted together. Stir in
the liqueur.

5 Remove the desserts from the heat, turn out onto
serving dishes, and pour over the sauce. Decorate
with coffee beans and serve.

cappuccino soufflé puddings

ingredients

serves 6

butter, for greasing
2 tbsp golden superfine sugar,
    plus extra for coating
⅓ cup whipping cream
2 tsp instant espresso coffee
    granules
2 tbsp Kahlúa
3 large eggs, separated,
    plus 1 extra egg white
5½ oz/150 g semisweet
    chocolate, melted and cooled
unsweetened cocoa, for dusting
chocolate-coated cookies,
    to serve

method

1 Lightly grease the sides of six ¾-cup ramekins with butter and coat with superfine sugar. Place the ramekins on a cookie sheet.

2 Place the cream in a small, heavy-bottom pan and heat gently. Stir in the coffee until it has dissolved, then stir in the Kahlúa. Divide the coffee mixture between the prepared ramekins.

3 Place the egg whites in a clean, greasefree bowl and whisk until soft peaks form, then gradually whisk in the sugar until stiff but not dry. Stir the egg yolks and melted chocolate together in a separate bowl, then stir in a little of the whisked egg whites. Gradually fold in the remaining egg whites.

4 Divide the mixture between the dishes. Bake in a preheated oven, 375°F/190°C, for 15 minutes, or until just set. Dust with unsweetened cocoa and serve immediately with chocolate-coated cookies.

chocolate zabaglione

ingredients

serves 4

4 egg yolks
generous ¼ cup superfine sugar
1¾ oz/50 g semisweet chocolate
½ cup Marsala wine
unsweetened cocoa, for dusting
amaretti cookies, to serve

method

1 Place the egg yolks and superfine sugar in a large glass bowl and, using an electric whisk, whisk together until the mixture is very pale.

2 Grate the chocolate finely and, using a spatula, fold into the egg mixture. Fold the Marsala wine into the chocolate mixture.

3 Place the bowl over a pan of gently simmering water and set the electric whisk on the lowest speed or swap to a balloon whisk. Cook gently, whipping constantly, until the mixture thickens. Do not overcook or the mixture will curdle.

4 Spoon the hot mixture into four warmed glass dishes or coffee cups and dust with cocoa. Serve as soon as possible, while it is warm, light, and fluffy, with amaretti cookies.

variation

Add 2 cups fresh strawberries, cut into quarters.
Pour the hot zabaglione over the strawberries and serve.

chocolate fondue

ingredients

serves 6

1 pineapple
1 mango
12 cape gooseberries
generous 1 cup fresh strawberries
generous 1½ cups seeded green
    grapes

fondue

9 oz/250 g semisweet chocolate,
    broken into pieces
⅔ cup heavy cream
2 tbsp brandy

method

1 Using a sharp knife, peel and core the pineapple, then cut the flesh into cubes. Peel the mango and cut the flesh into cubes. Peel back the papery outer skin of the cape gooseberries and twist at the top to make a "handle." Arrange all the fruit on six serving plates and let chill in the refrigerator.

2 To make the fondue, place the chocolate and cream in a fondue pot. Heat gently, stirring constantly, until the chocolate has melted. Stir in the brandy until blended and the chocolate mixture is smooth.

3 Place the fondue pot over the burner to keep warm. To serve, allow each guest to dip the fruit into the sauce, using fondue forks or bamboo skewers.

chilled & iced desserts

chocolate hazelnut parfaits

ingredients

serves 6

1½ cups blanched hazelnuts
6 oz/175 g semisweet chocolate,
　broken into small pieces
2½ cups heavy cream
2½ cups confectioners' sugar
3 eggs, separated
6 small fresh mint sprigs,
　to decorate
wafer cookies, to serve

method

1 Spread out the hazelnuts on a cookie sheet and toast under the broiler for about 5 minutes, shaking the sheet from time to time, until golden all over. Set aside to cool.

2 Put the chocolate in a heatproof bowl set over a saucepan of gently simmering water. Stir over low heat until melted, then remove from the heat and cool. Put the toasted hazelnuts in a food processor and process until finely ground.

3 Whip the cream until it is stiff, then fold in the ground hazelnuts and set aside. Add 3 tablespoons of the sugar to the egg yolks and beat for 10 minutes until pale and thick.

4 Whip the egg whites in a separate bowl until soft peaks form. Whisk in the remaining sugar, a little at a time, until the whites are stiff and glossy. Stir the cooled chocolate into the egg yolk mixture, then fold in the cream and finally, fold in the egg whites. Divide between six freezerproof timbales or molds, cover with plastic wrap, and freeze for at least 8 hours, until firm.

5 Transfer the parfaits to the refrigerator 10 minutes before serving to soften slightly. Turn out onto individual serving plates, decorate with mint sprigs, and serve with wafers.

chocolate & orange slices

ingredients

serves 8

unsalted butter, for greasing
14 oz/400 g semisweet
    chocolate, broken into pieces
3 small, loose-skinned citrus
    fruit such as oranges,
    tangerines, or mandarins
4 egg yolks
1 cup sour cream
2 tbsp raisins
1¼ cups whipped cream, to serve

method

1 Lightly grease a 1-lb/450-g terrine or loaf pan and line it with plastic wrap. Put the chocolate in a heatproof bowl set over a saucepan of gently simmering water. Stir over a low heat until melted. Remove from the heat and let cool slightly.

2 Meanwhile, peel the fruit, removing all traces of pith. Cut the zest into very thin strips. Beat the egg yolks into the chocolate, one at a time, then add most of the zest (reserve the rest for decoration) and all the sour cream and raisins, and beat until thoroughly combined. Spoon the mixture into the prepared loaf pan, cover with plastic wrap, and chill in the refrigerator for 3–4 hours, until set.

3 To serve, remove the loaf pan from the refrigerator and turn out the chocolate mold. Remove the plastic wrap and cut the mold into slices. Place a slice on individual serving plates and add whipped cream to serve. Decorate with the remaining zest.

white & dark chocolate ice cream

ingredients

serves 4

6 egg yolks
3½ cups superfine sugar
1½ cups milk
¾ cup heavy cream
3½ oz/100 g dark chocolate,
   chopped
3 oz/85 g white chocolate,
   grated or finely chopped
fresh mint leaves, to decorate

method

1 Put the egg yolks and sugar into a large, heatproof bowl and beat until fluffy. Heat the milk, cream, and dark chocolate in a saucepan over low heat, stirring, until melted and almost boiling. Remove from the heat and whisk into the egg mixture. Return to the saucepan and cook, stirring, over low heat until thick. Do not let it simmer. Transfer to a heatproof bowl and let cool. Cover the bowl with plastic wrap and chill in the refrigerator for 1½ hours. Remove from the refrigerator and stir in the white chocolate.

2 Transfer to a freezerproof container and freeze for 1 hour. Remove from the freezer, transfer to a bowl, and whisk to break up the ice crystals. Return to the container and freeze for 30 minutes. Repeat twice more, freezing for 30 minutes and whisking each time. Alternatively, transfer the mixture to an ice-cream machine and process for 15 minutes.

3 Scoop into serving bowls, decorate with mint leaves, and serve.

white chocolate terrine

ingredients

serves 8

2 tbsp granulated sugar
generous ¼ cup water
10 oz/280 g white chocolate
3 eggs, separated
1¼ cups heavy cream

to serve

fruit coulis
fresh strawberries

method

1 Line a 1-lb/450-g loaf pan with foil or plastic wrap, pressing out as many creases as you can.

2 Place the granulated sugar and water in a heavy-bottom saucepan and heat gently, stirring, until the sugar has dissolved. Bring to a boil and boil for 1–2 minutes until syrupy, then remove from the heat.

3 Break the white chocolate into small pieces and stir it into the hot syrup, continuing to stir until the chocolate has melted and combined with the syrup. Let the mixture cool slightly.

4 Beat the egg yolks into the chocolate mixture and let cool completely.

5 Lightly whip the cream until it is just holding its shape, and fold it into the chocolate mixture.

6 Whip the egg whites in a greasefree bowl until soft peaks form. Fold the whites into the chocolate mixture. Pour into the prepared loaf pan and freeze overnight.

7 To serve, remove the terrine from the freezer about 10–15 minutes before serving. Turn out of the pan and cut into slices. Serve with fruit coulis and strawberries.

chocolate & vanilla creams

ingredients

serves 4

2 cups heavy cream
generous ⅓ cup superfine sugar
1 vanilla bean
generous ¾ cup sour cream
2 tsp powdered gelatin
3 tbsp water
1¾ oz/50 g semisweet chocolate
chocolate shavings, to decorate

method

1 Place the cream and sugar in a saucepan, then add the vanilla bean. Heat gently, stirring until the sugar has dissolved, then bring to a boil. Reduce the heat and simmer for 2–3 minutes.

2 Remove the saucepan from the heat and take out the vanilla bean. Stir in the sour cream.

3 Sprinkle the gelatin over the water in a small heatproof bowl and let it get absorbed, then set over a saucepan of hot water and stir until dissolved. Stir into the cream mixture. Pour half of this mixture into another mixing bowl.

4 Put the semisweet chocolate in a heatproof bowl over a saucepan of gently simmering water until melted. Stir the melted chocolate into half of the cream mixture. Pour the chocolate mixture into four individual glass serving dishes and let chill for 15–20 minutes, until just set. While it is chilling, keep the vanilla mixture at room temperature.

5 Spoon the vanilla mixture on top of the chocolate mixture and let chill until the vanilla is set. Decorate with chocolate shavings.

brownie bottom cheesecake

ingredients

serves 12

brownie bottom layer

½ cup unsalted butter, plus extra
    for greasing
4 oz/115 g bittersweet chocolate,
    broken into pieces
1 cup superfine sugar
2 eggs, beaten
¼ cup milk
1 cup all-purpose flour, plus extra
    for dusting

topping

2¼ cups cream cheese or farmer's
    cheese
⅔ cup superfine sugar
3 eggs, beaten
1 tsp vanilla extract
½ cup plain yogurt
semisweet chocolate, melted,
    to drizzle

method

1 Lightly grease and flour a 9-inch/23-cm round
   springform cake pan.

2 Melt the butter and the chocolate in a pan over low
   heat, stirring frequently, until smooth. Remove from
   the heat and beat in the sugar.

3 Add the eggs and milk, beating well. Stir in the flour,
   mixing just until blended. Spoon into the prepared
   pan, spreading evenly.

4 Bake in a preheated oven, 350°F/180°C, for 25 minutes.
   Remove from the oven while preparing the topping.
   Reduce the oven temperature to 325°F/160°C.

5 For the topping, beat together the cream cheese,
   sugar, eggs, and vanilla extract until well blended.
   Stir in the yogurt, then pour over the brownie base.
   Bake for another 45–55 minutes, or until the center is
   almost set.

6 Run a knife around the edge of the cake to loosen
   from the pan. Let cool before removing from the pan.
   Chill in the refrigerator for 4 hours or overnight before
   cutting the cheesecake into slices. Serve drizzled with
   melted chocolate.

tiramisu layers

ingredients

serves 6

⅔ cup heavy cream
1¾ cups mascarpone cheese
10 oz/280 g semisweet chocolate,
    broken into pieces
1¼ cups hot black coffee
¼ cup superfine sugar
⅓ cup dark rum or cognac
54 ladyfingers
unsweetened cocoa, for dusting

method

1 Whip the cream until it just holds its shape. Beat the mascarpone to soften slightly, then fold in the whipped cream. Melt the chocolate in a heatproof bowl set over a saucepan of simmering water, stirring occasionally. Let the chocolate cool slightly, then stir it into the mascarpone and cream.

2 Mix the hot coffee and sugar in a saucepan and stir until dissolved. Let cool, then add the dark rum. Dip the ladyfingers into the mixture briefly so that they absorb the coffee and rum mixture, but do not become soggy.

3 Place 3 ladyfingers on each of six serving plates. Spoon a layer of the chocolate, mascarpone, and cream mixture over the ladyfingers.

4 Place 3 more ladyfingers crosswise on top of the chocolate and mascarpone mixture. Spread another layer of chocolate and mascarpone and place 3 more ladyfingers on top.

5 Let the tiramisu chill in the refrigerator for at least 1 hour. Dust with a little unsweetened cocoa just before serving.

chocolate & cherry tiramisu

ingredients

serves 4

generous ¾ cup strong black
coffee, cooled to room
temperature
⅓ cup cherry brandy
16 sponge cake squares
1¼ cups mascarpone
1¼ cups heavy cream, lightly
whipped
3 tbsp confectioner's sugar
9¼ oz/275 g sweet cherries,
halved and pitted

to decorate
chocolate curls
whole cherries

method

1 Pour the cooled coffee into a pitcher and stir in the
cherry brandy. Put half of the trifle sponges into a
serving dish, then pour over half of the coffee mixture.

2 Put the mascarpone into a separate bowl along with
the cream and sugar, and mix together well. Spread
half of the mascarpone mixture over the coffee-soaked
trifle sponges, then top with half of the cherries.
Arrange the remaining trifle sponges on top. Pour
over the remaining coffee mixture and top with the
remaining cherries. Finish with a layer of mascarpone
mixture. Cover with plastic wrap, and chill in the
refrigerator for at least 2 hours.

3 Remove from the refrigerator, decorate with the
chocolate curls and cherries, and serve.

marbled chocolate & orange ice cream

ingredients

serves 6

6 oz/175 g white chocolate
1 tsp cornstarch
1 tsp vanilla extract
3 egg yolks
1¼ cups milk
2 cups heavy cream
4 oz/115 g orange-flavored
    semisweet chocolate,
    broken into pieces
orange zest, to decorate
orange segments, to serve

method

1 Using a sharp knife, chop the white chocolate into small pieces and set aside. Beat the cornstarch, vanilla extract, and egg yolks in a heatproof bowl until well blended. Pour the milk into a large, heavy-bottom pan and bring to a boil over low heat. Pour the milk over the egg yolk mixture, stirring constantly.

2 Strain the mixture back into the pan and heat gently, stirring constantly, until thickened. Remove from the heat, add the white chocolate pieces and stir until melted. Stir in the cream. Set aside ²/₃ cup of the mixture and pour the remainder into a large freezer-proof container. Cover and freeze for 2 hours, or until starting to set. Melt the orange-flavored chocolate, stir into the reserved mixture and set aside.

3 Remove the partially frozen ice cream from the freezer and beat with a fork. Place spoonfuls of the orange chocolate mixture over the ice cream and swirl with a knife to give a marbled effect. Freeze for 8 hours, or overnight, until firm. Transfer to the refrigerator 30 minutes before serving. Scoop into individual glasses, decorate with orange rind, and serve with a few orange segments.

rich chocolate ice cream

ingredients

serves 6

1 egg
3 egg yolks
generous ½ cup superfine sugar
1¼ cups whole milk
9 oz/250 g semisweet chocolate
1¼ cups heavy cream

trellis cups

3½ oz/100 g semisweet chocolate

method

1 Beat the egg, egg yolks, and superfine sugar together in a mixing bowl until well combined. Heat the milk until it is almost boiling. Gradually pour the hot milk onto the eggs, whisking. Place the bowl over a pan of gently simmering water and cook, stirring constantly, until the custard mixture thickens sufficiently to thinly coat the back of a wooden spoon.

2 Break the chocolate into small pieces and add to the hot custard. Stir until the chocolate has melted. Cover and let cool.

3 Whip the cream until just holding its shape, then fold into the cooled chocolate custard. Transfer to a freezerproof container and freeze for 1–2 hours until the mixture is frozen 1 inch/2.5 cm from the sides. Scrape the ice cream into a chilled bowl and beat again until smooth. Re-freeze until firm.

4 To make the trellis cups, invert a muffin pan and cover six alternate mounds with plastic wrap. Melt the chocolate, place it in a paper pastry bag, and snip off the end. Pipe a circle around the bottom of the mound, then back and forth over it to form a double-thickness trellis. Pipe around the bottom again. Chill until set, lift from the pan and take off the plastic wrap. Serve the ice cream in the trellis cups.

coconut & white chocolate ice cream

serves 6

2 eggs
2 egg yolks
generous ½ cup golden superfine sugar
1¼ cups light cream
4 oz/115 g white chocolate, chopped
4 oz/115 g creamed coconut, chopped
1¼ cups heavy cream
3 tbsp coconut rum
tropical fruit, such as mango, pineapple, or passion fruit, to serve

method

1 Place the whole eggs, egg yolks, and sugar in a heatproof bowl and beat together until well blended. Place the light cream, chocolate, and coconut in a pan and heat gently until the chocolate has melted, then continue to heat, stirring constantly, until almost boiling. Pour onto the egg mixture, stirring vigorously, then set the bowl over a pan of gently simmering water, making sure that the base of the bowl does not touch the water.

2 Heat the mixture, stirring constantly, until it lightly coats the back of the spoon. Strain into a clean, heatproof bowl and let cool. Place the heavy cream and rum in a separate bowl and whip until slightly thickened, then fold into the cooled chocolate mixture.

3 Transfer to a freezerproof container and freeze for 1–2 hours until the mixture is frozen 1 inch/2.5 cm from the sides. Scrape the ice cream into a chilled bowl and beat again until smooth. Re-freeze until firm. Transfer the ice cream to the refrigerator for 30 minutes before serving. Scoop into small serving bowls and serve with tropical fruit.

white chocolate ice cream

ingredients

serves 6

ice cream

1 egg, plus 1 extra egg yolk
3 tbsp superfine sugar
5½ oz/150 g white chocolate
1¼ cups milk
⅔ cup heavy cream

cookie cups

1 egg white
2 oz/55 g superfine sugar
2 tbsp all-purpose flour, sifted
2 tbsp unsweetened cocoa, sifted
2 tbsp butter, melted
semisweet chocolate, melted,
    to serve

method

1 To make the ice cream, beat the egg, egg yolk, and sugar. Break the chocolate into pieces, place in a bowl with 3 tablespoons of milk, and melt over a pan of hot water. Heat the milk until almost boiling and pour onto the eggs, whisking. Place over a pan of simmering water and stir until the mixture thickens. Whip in the chocolate. Cover with dampened baking parchment and let cool.

2 Whip the cream and fold into the custard. Transfer to a freezerproof container and freeze the mixture for 1–2 hours until the mixture is frozen 1 inch/2.5 cm from the sides. Scrape into a chilled bowl and beat until smooth. Re-freeze until firm.

3 Line two cookie sheets with baking parchment. To make the cookie cups, beat the egg white and sugar. Beat in the flour and cocoa, then the butter. Place 1 tablespoon on one cookie sheet and spread out into a 5-inch/13-cm circle. Bake in a preheated oven, 400°F/200°C, for 4–5 minutes. Remove and mold over an upturned cup. Let set, then cool. Repeat to make six cookie cups. Serve the ice cream in the cookie cups, drizzled with melted chocolate.

sicilian cassata

ingredients

serves 8

generous 1 cup self-rising flour
2 tbsp unsweetened cocoa
1 tsp baking powder
¾ cup butter, softened, plus extra
for greasing
scant 1 cup golden superfine
sugar
3 eggs
confectioners' sugar, for dusting
chocolate curls, to decorate

filling

1 lb/450 g ricotta cheese
3½ oz/100 g semisweet chocolate,
grated
generous ½ cup golden superfine
sugar
3 tbsp Marsala wine
⅓ cup chopped candied peel
2 tbsp almonds, chopped

method

1 Grease and base-line a 7-inch/18-cm loose-baked
round tin. Sift the flour, unsweetened cocoa, and
baking powder into a large bowl. Add the butter, sugar,
and eggs and beat together thoroughly until smooth
and creamy. Pour the cake batter into the prepared
cake pan and bake in a preheated oven, 375°F/190°C,
for 30–40 minutes, or until well risen and firm to the
touch. Let stand in the pan for 5 minutes, then turn out
onto a wire rack to cool completely.

2 Wash and dry the cake pan and grease and line it again
To make the filling, rub the ricotta through a strainer
into a bowl. Add the grated chocolate, sugar, and
Marsala wine and beat together until the mixture is
light and fluffy. Stir in the candied peel and almonds.

3 Cut the thin crust off the top of the cake and discard.
Cut the cake horizontally into three layers. Place the
first slice in the prepared pan and cover with half the
ricotta mixture. Repeat the layers, finishing with a
cake layer. Press down lightly, cover with a plate and a
weight, and let chill in the refrigerator for 8 hours, or
overnight. To serve, turn the cake out onto a serving
plate. Dust with confectioners' sugar and decorate with
chocolate curls.

champagne mousses

ingredients

serves 4

sponge
4 eggs
½ cup superfine sugar
½ cup self-rising flour
2 tbsp unsweetened cocoa
2 tbsp butter, melted

mousse
1 envelope gelatin
3 tbsp water
1¼ cups champagne
1¼ cups heavy cream
2 egg whites
⅓ cup superfine sugar
2 oz/50 g semisweet
    chocolate-flavored cake
    covering, melted

method

1 Line a 15 x 10-inch/38 x 25-cm jelly roll pan with greased baking parchment. Place the eggs and sugar in a bowl and beat, using an electric mixer, until the mixture is very thick and the whisk leaves a trail when lifted. Sift the flour and cocoa together and fold into the egg mixture. Fold in the butter. Pour into the pan and bake in a preheated oven, 400°F/200°C, for 8 minutes, or until springy to the touch. Let cool for 5 minutes, then turn out onto a wire rack until cold. Meanwhile, line four 4-inch/10-cm baking rings with baking parchment. Line the sides with 1-inch/2.5-cm strips of cake and the bottom with circles.

2 For the mousse, sprinkle the gelatin over the water and let it go spongy. Place the bowl over a pan of hot water and stir until the gelatin has dissolved. Stir in the champagne.

3 Whip the cream until just holding its shape. Fold in the champagne mixture. Stand in a cool place until on the point of setting, stirring. Whip the egg whites until standing in soft peaks, add the sugar and whip until glossy. Fold the egg whites into the setting mixture. Spoon into the sponge cases, allowing the mixture to go above the sponge. Let chill in the refrigerator for 2 hours. Pipe the cake covering in squiggles, let them set, then use to decorate the mousses.

white chocolate molds

ingredients

serves 6

4½ oz/125 g white chocolate,
    broken into pieces
generous 1 cup heavy cream
3 tbsp sour cream
2 eggs, separated
3 tbsp water
1½ tsp powdered gelatin
oil, for brushing
1¼ cups sliced strawberries
1¼ cups raspberries
1¼ cups blueberries
scant ⅓ cup superfine sugar
½ cup crème de framboise

method

1 Put the chocolate in a heatproof bowl set over a pan of barely simmering water. Stir over a low heat until melted. Remove from the heat and set aside.

2 Pour the heavy cream into a pan and bring to just below boiling point over a low heat. Remove from the heat, then stir the cream and sour cream into the chocolate and let cool slightly. Beat in the egg yolks, one at a time.

3 Pour the water into a bowl and sprinkle over the gelatin. Let stand for 2–3 minutes to soften, then set over a pan of simmering water until dissolved. Stir into the chocolate mixture and let stand until nearly set.

4 Brush the insides of six timbales or ramekins with oil and line the bases with parchment paper. Whip the egg whites until soft peaks form, then fold them into the chocolate mixture. Divide the mixture among the molds and smooth the surface. Cover with plastic wrap and let chill for 2 hours, until set.

5 Put the strawberries, raspberries, and blueberries in a bowl. Sprinkle with the superfine sugar, then stir in the liqueur. Cover with plastic wrap and let chill for 2 hours.

6 To serve, turn out onto individual plates. Divide the fruit among the plates and serve.

chocolate & orange pots

ingredients

serves 8

7 oz/200 g plain chocolate,
    broken into pieces
grated rind of 1 orange
1¼ cups heavy cream
¾ cup golden superfine sugar
3 tbsp Cointreau
3 large egg whites
orange zest, to decorate
crisp biscuits, to serve

method

1 Melt the chocolate and stir in the orange rind. Place the cream in a bowl with ½ cup of the sugar and the Cointreau and whip until thick.

2 Place the egg whites in a clean and greasefree bowl and whip until soft peaks form, then gradually whip in the remaining sugar until stiff but not dry. Fold the melted chocolate into the cream, then beat in a spoonful of the whisked egg whites. Gently fold in the remaining egg whites until thoroughly mixed.

3 Spoon the mixture into eight small ramekin dishes or demi-tasse coffee cups. Cover and leave to chill in the refrigerator for 1 hour, then decorate with a few strips of orange rind before serving with crisp biscuits.

coffee panna cotta with chocolate sauce

ingredients

serves 6

oil, for brushing
2½ cups heavy cream
1 vanilla bean
generous ¼ cup golden
    superfine sugar
2 tsp instant espresso coffee
    granules, dissolved in
    4 tbsp water
2 tsp powdered gelatin

sauce
⅔ cup light cream
2 oz/55 g semisweet chocolate,
    melted

to decorate
chocolate-covered coffee beans
cocoa, for dusting

method

1 Lightly brush six 5-fl oz/150 ml molds with oil. Place the cream in a saucepan. Split the vanilla pod and scrape the black seeds into the cream. Add the vanilla bean and the sugar, then heat gently until almost boiling. Strain the cream into a heatproof bowl and reserve. Place the coffee in a small heatproof bowl, sprinkle on the gelatin and leave for 5 minutes, or until spongy. Set the bowl over a saucepan of gently simmering water until the gelatin has dissolved.

2 Stir a little of the reserved cream into the gelatin mixture, then stir the gelatin mixture into the remainder of the cream. Divide the mixture among the prepared molds and let cool, then leave to chill in the refrigerator for 8 hours, or overnight.

3 To make the sauce, place one-quarter of the cream in a bowl and stir in the melted chocolate. Gradually stir in the remaining cream, reserving 1 tablespoon. To serve the panna cotta, dip the bases of the molds briefly into hot water and turn out onto six dessert plates. Pour the chocolate cream around. Dot drops of the reserved cream onto the sauce and feather it with a skewer. Decorate with chocolate-covered coffee beans and cocoa. Serve immediately.

chocolate marquise

ingredients

serves 6

7 oz/200 g semisweet chocolate
generous ⅓ cup butter
3 egg yolks
scant ⅓ cup superfine sugar
1 tsp chocolate extract or
   1 tbsp chocolate-flavored
   liqueur
1¼ cups heavy cream

to serve

chocolate-dipped fruits
sour cream
unsweetened cocoa, for dusting

method

1 Break the chocolate into pieces. Place the chocolate and butter in a bowl set over a pan of gently simmering water and stir until melted and well combined. Remove the pan from the heat and let the chocolate cool.

2 Place the egg yolks in a mixing bowl with the sugar and whip until pale and fluffy. Using an electric mixer running on low speed, slowly whip in the cool chocolate mixture. Stir in the chocolate extract or chocolate-flavored liqueur.

3 Whip the cream until just holding its shape. Fold into the chocolate mixture. Spoon into six small custard pots or individual metal molds. Chill the desserts in the refrigerator for at least 2 hours.

4 To serve, turn out the desserts onto individual serving dishes. If you have difficulty turning them out, first dip the pots or molds into a bowl of warm water for a few seconds. Serve with chocolate-dipped fruits and sour cream and dust with cocoa.

irish cream cheesecake

ingredients

serves 12

oil, for brushing
6 oz/175 g chocolate chip cookies
¼ cup butter

filling

8 oz/225 g semisweet chocolate,
    broken into pieces
8 oz/225 g milk chocolate,
    broken into pieces
generous ¼ cup golden
    superfine sugar
1½ cups cream cheese
1¾ cups heavy cream, whipped
3 tbsp Irish cream liqueur

to serve

sour cream
fresh fruit

method

1 Line the base of an 8-inch/20-cm springform pan with foil and brush the sides with oil.

2 Place the cookies in a plastic bag and crush with a rolling pin. Place the butter in a saucepan and heat gently until just melted, then stir in the crushed cookies. Press the mixture into the base of the pan and let chill in the refrigerator for 1 hour.

3 To make the filling, melt the semisweet and milk chocolate together, stir to combine and leave to cool. Place the sugar and cream cheese in a large bowl and beat together until smooth, then fold in the whipped cream. Fold the mixture gently into the melted chocolate, then stir in the Irish cream liqueur.

4 Spoon the filling over the chilled cookie base and smooth the surface. Cover and leave to chill in the refrigerator for 2 hours, or until quite firm to the touch. Transfer to a serving plate and cut into small slices. Serve with a spoonful of sour cream and fresh fruit.

chocolate terrine with orange cream

ingredients

serves 10–12

1/3 cup water
3 tsp powdered gelatin
4 oz/115 g each of milk, white, and semisweet chocolate, broken into pieces
2 cups whipping cream
6 eggs, separated
scant 1/2 cup superfine sugar

orange cream

2 tbsp superfine sugar
1 tbsp cornstarch
2 egg yolks
2/3 cup milk
2/3 cup heavy cream
grated rind of 1 orange
1 tbsp Cointreau

to decorate

2/3 cup heavy cream, whipped
chocolate-covered coffee beans
orange zest

method

1 To make the milk chocolate mousse, place 2 tablespoons of the water in a heatproof bowl. Sprinkle on 1 teaspoon of gelatin and let stand for 5 minutes. Set the bowl over a pan of simmering water until the gelatin has dissolved. Let cool. Melt the milk chocolate and let cool. Whip one-third of the cream until thick. Whisk two of the egg whites in a bowl until stiff but not dry. Whisk two of the egg yolks and one-third of the sugar in a separate bowl until thick. Stir in the chocolate, gelatin, and whipped cream. Fold in the whisked egg whites.

2 Pour into a 5-cup loaf pan, lined with plastic wrap. Cover and freeze for 20 minutes. Make the white chocolate mousse, pour over the milk chocolate mousse and freeze. Make the semisweet chocolate mousse and pour on top. Chill in the refrigerator for 2 hours, until set.

3 To make the orange cream, stir the sugar, cornstarch, and egg yolks together until smooth. Heat the milk, cream, and orange rind until almost boiling, then whisk into the egg mixture. Strain back into the pan and heat until thick. Cover and let cool, then stir in the Cointreau. Turn out and decorate with cream, coffee beans, and orange zest. Serve with the orange cream.

cakes & tortes

chocolate brownie cake

ingredients

serves 10

scant 1 cup butter
4 oz/115 g semisweet chocolate,
    broken into pieces
1¼ cups granulated sugar
½ cup light brown sugar
4 eggs, beaten
¾ cup all-purpose flour
1 tsp vanilla extract
pinch of salt
½ cup dried cranberries
scant ½ cup toasted slivered
    almonds, plus extra
    to decorate

frosting

4 oz/115 g semisweet chocolate,
    broken into pieces
2 tbsp butter
2 cups confectioners' sugar
2 fl oz/60 ml milk

method

1 Lightly grease and line the bottoms of two 7-inch/
   18-cm round shallow cake pans with parchment pape

2 Place the butter in a heavy-bottom pan and add the
   chocolate. Heat gently, stirring frequently, until the
   mixture has melted. Remove from the heat and stir
   until smooth. Add the sugars, stir well, then let cool
   for 10 minutes.

3 Gradually add the eggs to the cooled chocolate
   mixture, beating well after each addition. Stir in the
   flour, vanilla extract, and salt. Stir in the cranberries
   and slivered almonds, mix, then divide between the
   prepared cake pans.

4 Bake in a preheated oven, 350°F/180°C, for 25–30
   minutes, or until springy to the touch. Remove from
   the oven and let cool slightly in the pans before
   turning out onto a wire rack to cool completely.

5 To make the frosting, melt the chocolate and butter in
   a heavy-bottom pan and stir until smooth. Gradually
   beat in the confectioners' sugar with enough milk to
   create a smooth spreading consistency. Use some of
   the frosting to sandwich the two cakes together, then
   spread the top and sides with the remainder, swirling
   the top to create a decorative effect. Sprinkle with
   slivered almonds. Let the frosting set before serving.

dark & white fudge cupcakes

ingredients

makes 20

scant 1 cup water
5 tbsp unsalted butter
⅓ cup superfine sugar
1 tbsp corn syrup
3 tbsp milk
1 tsp vanilla extract
1 tsp baking soda
1½ cups all-purpose flour
2 tbsp unsweetened cocoa

topping

1¾ oz/50 g semisweet chocolate
4 tbsp water
¼ cup unsalted butter
1¾ oz/50 g white chocolate
3 cups confectioners' sugar

to decorate

3½ oz/100 g semisweet
   chocolate shavings
3½ oz/100 g white chocolate
   shavings

method

1 Put 20 paper baking cases in two muffin pans, or put 20 double-layer paper cases on two cookie sheets.

2 Put the water, butter, superfine sugar, and corn syrup in a saucepan. Heat gently, stirring, until the sugar has dissolved, then bring to a boil. Reduce the heat and cook for 5 minutes. Remove from the heat and let coo

3 Meanwhile, put the milk and vanilla extract in a bowl. Add the baking soda and stir to dissolve. Sift the flour and cocoa into a separate bowl and add the corn syrup mixture. Stir in the milk and beat until smooth. Spoon the batter into the paper cases until they are two-thirds full.

4 Bake the cupcakes in a preheated oven, 350°F/180°C, for 20 minutes, or until well risen and firm to the touch Transfer to a wire rack and let cool.

5 To make the topping, break the semisweet chocolate into a small heatproof bowl, add half the water and half the butter, and set the bowl over a pan of gently simmering water until melted. Stir until smooth and le stand over the water. Repeat with the white chocolate and remaining water and butter. Sift half the sugar into each bowl and beat until smooth and thick. Top the cupcakes with the frostings. Let set. Serve decorated with chocolate shavings.

blackberry chocolate flan

ingredients

serves 6

pie dough

1 cup all-purpose flour, plus
　　extra for dusting
¼ cup unsweetened cocoa
½ cup confectioners' sugar
pinch of salt
scant ¾ cup unsalted butter,
　　cut into small pieces
½ egg yolk

filling

1¼ cups heavy cream
6 oz/175 g blackberry jelly
8 oz/225 g semisweet chocolate,
　　broken into pieces
2 tbsp unsalted butter, cut into
　　small pieces

sauce

4 cups blackberries,
　　plus extra for decoration
1 tbsp lemon juice
2 tbsp superfine sugar
2 tbsp crème de cassis

method

1 To make the pie dough, first sift the flour, cocoa,
sugar, and salt into a food processor. Add the butter
and egg yolk and gradually mix these into the dry
ingredients. Knead lightly and form into a ball. Wrap
in plastic wrap and let chill in the refrigerator for 1 hour.

2 Roll out the dough on a lightly floured counter. Use it
to line a 12 x 4-inch/30 x 10-cm rectangular flan pan
and prick the pie shell with a fork. Line the bottom with
parchment paper and fill with dried beans or baking
beans. Bake in a preheated oven, 350°F/180°C, for
15 minutes. Remove the flan from the oven and take
out the paper and beans. Set aside to cool.

3 To make the filling, place the cream and jelly in a
saucepan and bring to a boil over low heat. Remove
from the heat and stir in the chocolate and then the
butter until melted and smooth. Pour the mixture into
the pie shell and set aside to cool.

4 To make the sauce, put the blackberries, lemon juice,
and superfine sugar in a food processor and process
until smooth. Strain through a nylon sieve and stir in
the cassis. Set aside. Remove the flan from the pan and
place on a serving plate. Arrange the blackberries on
top and brush with the blackberry and liqueur sauce.
Serve the flan with the remaining sauce on the side.

devil's food cake

ingredients

serves 10–12

3½ oz/100 g semisweet chocolate,
    broken into pieces
generous 1½ cups self-rising flour
1 tsp baking soda
1 cup butter, plus extra
    for greasing
2 cups dark brown sugar
1 tsp vanilla extract
3 eggs
½ cup buttermilk
1 cup boiling water

frosting

1½ cups superfine sugar
2 egg whites
1 tbsp lemon juice
3 tbsp orange juice
candied orange peel,
    to decorate

method

1 Lightly grease and base-line two 8-inch/20-cm shallow
   round cake pans.

2 Melt the chocolate in a heatproof bowl over a pan
   of simmering water. Sift the flour and baking soda
   together into a bowl.

3 Place the butter and sugar in a large bowl and beat
   until pale and fluffy. Beat in the vanilla extract and the
   eggs, one at a time, beating well after each addition.
   Add a little flour if the mixture starts to curdle. Fold the
   melted chocolate into the mixture until well blended.
   Fold in the remaining flour, then stir in the buttermilk
   and the boiling water.

4 Divide the mixture between the prepared pans. Bake in
   a preheated oven, 375°F/190°C, for 30 minutes, or until
   springy to the touch. Let cool in the pans for 5 minutes,
   then transfer to a wire rack and let cool completely.

5 Place the frosting ingredients in a large bowl set over a
   pan of simmering water. Using an electric whisk, whip
   until thick and forming soft peaks. Remove from the
   heat and whip until the mixture is cool.

6 Sandwich the two cakes together with a little of the
   frosting, then spread the remainder over the sides and
   top of the cake. Decorate with candied orange peel.

mocha layer cake

ingredients

serves 8

generous 1½ cups self-rising flour
¼ tsp baking powder
1 cup unsweetened cocoa
½ cup superfine sugar
2 eggs
2 tbsp corn syrup
⅔ cup corn oil
⅔ cup milk
butter for greasing

filling

1 tsp instant coffee
1 tbsp boiling water
1¼ cups heavy cream
2 tbsp confectioners' sugar

to decorate

1¾ oz/50 g semisweet chocolate, grated
chocolate caraque
confectioners' sugar, for dusting

method

1 Sift the flour, baking powder, and cocoa into a large bowl, then stir in the sugar. Make a well in the center and stir in the eggs, syrup, corn oil, and milk. Beat with a wooden spoon, gradually mixing in the dry ingredients to make a smooth batter. Divide the mixture between three lightly greased 7-inch/18-cm shallow, round cake pans.

2 Bake in a preheated oven, 350°F/180°C, for 35–45 minutes, or until springy to the touch. Let stand in the pans for 5 minutes, then turn out and let cool completely on a wire rack.

3 To make the filling, dissolve the instant coffee in the boiling water and place in a large bowl with the cream and confectioners' sugar. Whip until the cream is just holding its shape, then use half the cream to sandwich the three cakes together. Spread the remaining cream over the top and sides of the cake. Press the grated chocolate into the cream round the edge of the cake.

4 Transfer the cake to a serving plate. Lay the chocolate caraque over the top of the cake. Cut a few thin strips of parchment paper and place on top of the chocolate caraque. Dust lightly with confectioners' sugar, then carefully remove the paper. Serve.

chocolate ganache cake

ingredients

serves 10

¾ cup butter, plus extra for
    greasing
¾ cup superfine sugar
4 eggs, lightly beaten
1¾ cups self-rising flour
1 tbsp unsweetened cocoa
1¾ oz/50 g semisweet chocolate,
    melted

ganache

2 cups heavy cream
13 oz/375 g semisweet chocolate,
    broken into pieces
7 oz/200 g chocolate-flavored
    cake covering, to finish

method

1 Lightly grease and base-line an 8-inch/20-cm springform
   cake pan. Beat the butter and sugar until light and
   fluffy. Gradually add the eggs, beating well. Sift the flour
   and cocoa together. Fold into the cake mixture. Fold in
   the melted chocolate. Spoon into the cake pan.

2 Bake in a preheated oven, 350°F/180°C, for 40 minutes,
   or until springy to the touch. Let cool for 5 minutes
   in the pan, then turn out onto a wire rack to cool
   completely. Cut the cold cake into two layers.

3 To make the ganache, place the cream in a pan and
   bring to a boil, stirring. Add the chocolate and stir until
   melted and combined. Pour into a bowl and whip for
   about 5 minutes, or until fluffy and cool. Set aside
   one-third of the ganache and use the rest to sandwich
   the cake together and spread smoothly and evenly
   over the top and sides of the cake.

4 Melt the cake covering and spread it over a large sheet
   of baking parchment. Let cool until just set. Cut into
   strips a little wider than the height of the cake. Place
   them around the edge of the cake, overlapping slightly.

5 Using a pastry bag fitted with a fine tip, pipe the
   reserved ganache in tear drops or shells to cover
   the top of the cake. Let chill in the refrigerator for
   1 hour before serving.

white truffle cake

ingredients

serves 12

2 eggs
generous ¼ cup superfine sugar
generous ⅓ cup all-purpose flour
1¾ oz/50 g white chocolate,
    melted

truffle topping

1¼ cups heavy cream
12 oz/350 g white chocolate,
    broken into pieces
generous 1 cup mascarpone
    cheese

to decorate

semisweet, light, or white
    chocolate caraque
unsweetened cocoa, for dusting

method

1 Lightly grease and line an 8-inch/20-cm round
   springform cake pan. Whip the eggs and superfine
   sugar in a mixing bowl for 10 minutes, or until the
   mixture is very light and foamy and the whisk leaves
   a trail that lasts a few seconds when lifted. Sift the flour
   and fold in with a metal spoon. Fold in the melted
   white chocolate.

2 Pour into the prepared pan and bake in a preheated
   oven, 350°F/180°C, for 25 minutes, or until springy
   to the touch. Let cool slightly, then transfer to a wire
   rack to cool completely. Wash and dry the cake pan
   and return the cold cake to the pan, again lined
   and greased.

3 To make the topping, place the cream in a pan and
   bring to a boil, stirring to prevent it sticking to the
   bottom of the pan. Cool slightly, then add the white
   chocolate pieces and stir until melted and combined.
   Remove from the heat and stir until almost cool, then
   stir in the mascarpone cheese. Pour the mixture on
   top of the cake and let chill in the refrigerator for
   2 hours before serving.

4 Remove the cake from the pan and transfer to a plate.
   Decorate the top of the cake with the caraque. Dust
   with cocoa powder. Serve.

double chocolate gâteau

ingredients

serves 10

filling
generous 1 cup whipping cream
8 oz/225 g white chocolate

sponge
1 cup butter, softened, plus extra
    for greasing
generous 1 cup golden superfine
    sugar
4 eggs, beaten
generous 1 cup self-rising flour
½ cup unsweetened cocoa

frosting
12 oz/350 g semisweet chocolate
½ cup butter
⅓ cup heavy cream

to decorate
chocolate curls, chilled
4 oz/115 g semisweet chocolate,
    broken into pieces
2 tsp confectioners' sugar and
    unsweetened cocoa

method

1 To make the filling, heat the cream to almost boiling.
   Place the white chocolate in a food processor and
   chop coarsely. With the motor running, pour the cream
   through the feed tube. Process for 10–15 seconds, or
   until the mixture is smooth. Transfer to a bowl and let
   cool. Cover and let chill for 2 hours, or until firm to the
   touch. Whip until just starting to hold soft peaks.

2 Lightly grease and base-line an 8-inch/20-cm deep
   round cake pan. To make the sponge, beat the butter
   and sugar together until light and fluffy. Gradually beat
   in the eggs. Sift the flour and cocoa into another bowl,
   then fold into the batter. Spoon the mixture into the
   prepared pan and level the surface. Bake in a preheated
   oven, 350°F/180°C, for 45–50 minutes, or until springy
   to the touch and the tip of a knife inserted into the
   center comes out clean. Let stand in the pan for
   5 minutes, then let cool on a wire rack.

3 To make the frosting, break and melt the chocolate.
   Stir in the butter and cream. Let cool, stirring frequently,
   until the mixture is a spreading consistency. Slice the
   cake into three layers. Sandwich the layers together
   with the filling. Cover the cake with frosting and put
   chocolate curls on top. Mix together the confectioners'
   sugar and cocoa and sift over the cake. Serve.

double chocolate roulade

ingredients

serves 8

4 eggs, separated
generous ½ cup golden superfine
    sugar
4 oz/115 g semisweet chocolate,
    melted and cooled
1 tsp instant coffee granules,
    dissolved in 2 tbsp hot
    water, cooled
confectioners' sugar, to decorate
unsweetened cocoa, for dusting
fresh raspberries, to serve

filling

generous 1 cup whipping cream
5 oz/140 g white chocolate,
    broken into pieces
3 tbsp Tia Maria

method

1 Line a 9 x 13-inch/23 x 33-cm jelly roll pan with nonstick parchment paper. Whip the egg yolks and sugar in a bowl until pale and mousse-like. Fold in the chocolate, then the coffee. Place the egg whites in a clean bowl and whip until stiff but not dry. Stir a little of the egg whites into the chocolate mixture, then fold in the remainder. Pour into the pan and bake in a preheated oven, 350°F/180°C, for 15–20 minutes, or until firm to the touch. Cover with a damp dish towel and let stand in the pan for 8 hours, or overnight.

2 Meanwhile, make the filling. Heat the cream until almost boiling. Place the chocolate in a food processor and chop coarsely. With the motor running, pour the cream through the feed tube. Process until smooth. Stir in the Tia Maria. Transfer to a bowl and let cool. Let chill in the refrigerator for 8 hours, or overnight.

3 To assemble the roulade, whip the chocolate cream until soft peaks form. Cut a sheet of waxed paper larger than the roulade, place on a counter and sift confectioners' sugar over it. Turn the roulade out onto the paper. Peel away the lining paper. Spread the chocolate cream over the roulade and roll up from the short side nearest to you. Transfer to a dish, seam-side down. Let chill in the refrigerator for 2 hours, then dust with cocoa. Serve with raspberries.

chocolate & orange cake

ingredients

serves 8

generous ¾ cup superfine sugar
¾ cup butter
3 eggs, beaten
scant 1¼ cups self-rising flour,
    sifted
2 tbsp unsweetened cocoa, sifted
2 tbsp milk
3 tbsp orange juice
grated rind of ½ orange

frosting

1½ cups confectioners' sugar
2 tbsp orange juice
a little melted chocolate

method

1 Lightly grease an 8-inch/20-cm deep round cake pan.
   Beat the sugar and butter together in a bowl until light
   and fluffy. Gradually add the eggs, beating well after
   each addition. Carefully fold in the flour. Divide the
   mixture in half. Add the cocoa and milk to one half,
   stirring until well combined. Flavor the other half with
   the orange juice and grated orange rind.

2 Place spoonfuls of each mixture into the prepared
   pan and swirl together with a skewer, to create a
   marbled effect. Bake in a preheated oven, 375°F/190°C,
   for 25 minutes, or until the cake is springy to the
   touch. Let cool in the pan for a few minutes before
   transferring to a wire rack to cool completely.

3 To make the frosting, sift the confectioners' sugar into
   a mixing bowl and mix in enough of the orange juice to
   form a smooth frosting. Spread the frosting over
   the top of the cake and leave to set. Pipe fine lines of
   melted chocolate over the top, then drag a toothpick
   in the opposite direction to create a feathered effect.
   Let set before serving.

date & chocolate cake

ingredients

serves 6

4 oz/115 g semisweet chocolate
1 tbsp grenadine
1 tbsp corn syrup
½ cup unsalted butter, plus extra
　for greasing
generous ¼ cup superfine sugar
2 large eggs
generous ½ cup self-rising flour,
　plus extra for dusting
2 tbsp ground rice
1 tbsp confectioners' sugar,
　to decorate

filling

⅔ cup chopped dried dates
1 tbsp orange juice
1 tbsp raw sugar
⅛ cup blanched almonds,
　chopped
2 tbsp apricot jelly

method

1 Lightly grease 2 x 7-inch/18-cm sandwich cake pans, and dust with flour.

2 Break the chocolate into pieces, then place the chocolate, grenadine, and syrup in the top of a double boiler or in a heatproof bowl set over a pan of barely simmering water. Stir over low heat until the chocolate has melted and the mixture is smooth. Remove the pan from the heat and let cool.

3 Beat the butter and superfine sugar together in a bowl until pale and fluffy. Gradually beat in the eggs, then beat in the chocolate mixture. Sift the flour into another bowl and stir in the ground rice. Fold the 2 mixtures together.

4 Divide the cake batter between the prepared pans and level the surfaces. Bake in a preheated oven, 350°F/180°C, for 20–25 minutes, or until golden and firm to the touch. Turn out onto a wire rack to cool.

5 To make the filling, put all the ingredients into a pan and stir over low heat for 4–5 minutes, or until fully blended. Remove from the heat, let cool, then use the filling to sandwich the cakes together. Dust the top of the cake with confectioners' sugar and serve.

chocolate marshmallow cake

ingredients

serves 6

scant ³/₄ cup unsalted butter,
    plus extra for greasing
generous 1 cup superfine sugar
¹/₂ tsp vanilla extract
2 eggs, lightly beaten
3 oz/85 g semisweet chocolate,
    broken into pieces
²/₃ cup buttermilk
1¹/₄ cups self-rising flour
¹/₂ tsp baking soda
pinch of salt

frosting

1 tbsp milk
6 oz/175 g white marshmallows
2 egg whites
2 tbsp superfine sugar
2 oz/55 g milk chocolate, grated,
    to decorate

method

1 Lightly grease a 3¹/₂-cup ovenproof bowl. Cream the
  butter, sugar, and vanilla together in a bowl until pale
  and fluffy, then gradually beat in the eggs.

2 Melt the chocolate in a bowl over a pan of simmering
  water. Stir in the buttermilk gradually until well
  combined. Let cool slightly.

3 Sift the flour, baking soda, and salt into a separate bowl.
  Add the chocolate and the flour mixtures alternately
  to the creamed mixture, a little at a time. Spoon the
  mixture into the prepared bowl and smooth the
  surface. Bake in a preheated oven, 325°F/160°C, for
  50 minutes, until a skewer inserted into the center of the
  cake comes out clean. Turn out onto a wire rack to cool.

4 Meanwhile, make the frosting. Heat the milk and
  marshmallows very gently in a small pan until the
  marshmallows have melted. Remove from the heat
  and let cool. Whip the egg whites until soft peaks form,
  then add the sugar and continue whipping, until stiff
  peaks form. Fold into the cooled marshmallow mixture
  and set aside for 10 minutes.

5 When the cake is cool, cover the top and sides with
  the marshmallow frosting. Top with grated milk
  chocolate. Serve.

family chocolate cake

ingredients

serves 8

½ cup soft margarine, plus extra
　for greasing
generous ½ cup superfine sugar
2 eggs
1 tbsp light corn syrup
1 cup self-rising flour, sifted
2 tbsp unsweetened cocoa,
　sifted

filling and topping

4 tbsp confectioners' sugar, sifted
2 tbsp butter
3½ oz/100 g white or milk cooking
　chocolate
a little milk or white chocolate,
　melted

method

1 Lightly grease 2 x 7-inch/18-cm shallow cake pans.
Place all of the ingredients for the cake in a large mixing
bowl and beat with a wooden spoon or electric mixer
to form a smooth mixture.

2 Divide the mixture between the pans and smooth
the tops. Bake in a preheated oven, 375°F/190°C, for
20 minutes, or until springy to the touch. Cool for a few
minutes in the pans then transfer the cakes to a wire
rack to cool completely.

3 To make the filling, beat the sugar and butter together
in a bowl until light and fluffy. Melt the white or light
cooking chocolate and beat half into the icing mixture.
Use the filling to sandwich the two cakes together.

4 Spread the remaining melted cooking chocolate over
the top of the cake. Pipe circles of contrasting light
or white chocolate and feather into the cooking
chocolate with a toothpick, if desired. Let the cake
set before serving.

mocha cupcakes with whipped cream

ingredients

makes 20

2 tbsp instant espresso
    coffee powder
scant ¼ cup butter
½ cup superfine sugar
1 tbsp honey
generous 1 cup water
generous 1½ cups all-purpose flour
2 tbsp unsweetened cocoa
1 tsp baking soda
3 tbsp milk
1 large egg, lightly beaten

topping

1 cup whipping cream
unsweetened cocoa, sifted,
    for dusting

method

1 Put 20 paper baking cases in two muffin pans, or put 20 double-layer paper cases on two cookie sheets.

2 Put the coffee powder, butter, sugar, honey, and water in a pan and heat gently, stirring, until the sugar has dissolved. Bring to a boil, then reduce the heat and let simmer for 5 minutes. Pour into a large heatproof bowl and let cool.

3 When the mixture has cooled, sift in the flour and cocoa. Dissolve the baking soda in the milk, then add to the mixture with the egg and beat together until smooth. Spoon the batter into the paper cases.

4 Bake the cupcakes in a preheated oven, 350°F/180°C, for 15–20 minutes, or until well risen and firm to the touch. Transfer to a wire rack to cool completely.

5 For the topping, whip the cream in a bowl until it holds its shape. Just before serving, spoon teaspoonfuls of cream on top of each cake, then dust lightly with sifted cocoa. Store the cupcakes in the refrigerator until ready to serve.

warm molten-centered chocolate cupcakes

ingredients

makes 8

4 tbsp soft margarine
generous ¼ cup superfine sugar
1 large egg
generous ½ cup self-rising flour
1 tbsp unsweetened cocoa
2 oz/55 g semisweet chocolate
confectioners' sugar,
    for dusting

method

1 Put 8 paper baking cases in a muffin pan, or place 8 double-layer paper cases on a cookie sheet.

2 Put the margarine, sugar, egg, flour, and cocoa in a large bowl and, using an electric hand whisk, beat together until just smooth.

3 Spoon half of the batter into the paper cases. Using a teaspoon, make an indentation in the center of each cake. Break the chocolate evenly into 8 squares and place a piece in each indentation, then spoon the remaining cake batter on top.

4 Bake the cupcakes in a preheated oven, 375°F/190°C for 20 minutes, or until well risen and springy to the touch. Let stand for 2–3 minutes before serving warm, dusted with sifted confectioners' sugar.

dark & white chocolate torte

ingredients

serves 6

4 eggs
½ cup superfine sugar
¾ cup all-purpose flour
butter, for greasing

filling

1¼ cups heavy cream
5½ oz/150 g semisweet chocolate,
broken into small pieces

topping

2¾ oz/75 g white chocolate
1 tbsp butter
1 tbsp milk
2 oz/55 g confectioners' sugar
shavings of chocolate, to decorate

method

1 Lightly grease and base-line an 8-inch/20-cm round springform cake pan. Whip the eggs and superfine sugar in a large bowl with an electric whisk for 10 minutes, or until the mixture is very light and foamy and the whisk leaves a trail that lasts a few seconds when lifted.

2 Sift the flour and fold in with a metal spoon or spatula. Pour into the prepared pan and bake in a preheated oven, 350°F/180°C, for 35–40 minutes, or until springy to the touch. Let cool slightly, then transfer to a wire rack to cool completely.

3 For the filling, place the cream in a pan and bring to a boil, stirring. Add the chocolate and stir until melted. Remove from the heat, transfer to a bowl, and let cool. Beat with a wooden spoon until thick.

4 Slice the cold cake horizontally into two layers. Sandwich the layers together with the semisweet chocolate cream and place on a wire rack.

5 For the topping, melt the chocolate and butter together and stir until blended. Whip in the milk and confectioners' sugar. Continue whipping for a few minutes, until the frosting is cool. Pour it over the cake and spread with a spatula to coat the top and sides. Let set before decorating with chocolate shavings.

chocolate & almond torte

ingredients

serves 10

8 oz/225 g semisweet chocolate,
    broken into pieces
3 tbsp water
¼ cup brown sugar
¾ cup butter, softened, plus extra
    for greasing
¼ cup ground almonds
3 tbsp self-rising flour
5 eggs, separated
⅔ cup finely chopped blanched
    almonds
confectioners' sugar, for dusting
fresh berries and heavy cream,
    to serve

method

1 Lightly grease and line a 9-inch/23-cm loose-bottom cake pan. Melt the chocolate with the water in a pan set over very low heat, stirring until smooth. Add the sugar and stir until dissolved, taking the pan off the heat to prevent it overheating.

2 Add the butter in small amounts until it has melted into the chocolate. Remove from the heat and lightly stir in the ground almonds and flour. Add the egg yolks one at a time, beating well after each addition.

3 Whip the egg whites in a large mixing bowl, until they stand in soft peaks, then fold them into the chocolate mixture with a metal spoon. Stir in the chopped almonds. Pour the mixture into the prepared pan and smooth the surface.

4 Bake in a preheated oven, 350°F/180°C, for 40–45 minutes, or until well risen and firm to the touch (the cake will crack on the surface during cooking).

5 Let cool in the pan for 30–40 minutes, then turn out onto a wire rack to cool completely. Dust with confectioners' sugar and serve in slices with fresh berries and cream.

chocolate truffle torte

ingredients

serves 10

generous ¼ cup golden superfine
    sugar
2 eggs
scant ¼ cup all-purpose flour
¼ cup unsweetened cocoa,
    plus extra for decorating
butter, for greasing
¼ cup cold strong black coffee
2 tbsp brandy

topping

2½ cups whipping cream
15 oz/425 g semisweet chocolate,
    melted and cooled
confectioners' sugar,
    to decorate

method

1 Lightly grease and base-line a 9-inch/23-cm springform
cake pan. Place the sugar and eggs in a heatproof bowl
and set over a pan of hot water. Whip together until
pale and mousse-like. Sift the flour and unsweetened
cocoa into a separate bowl, then fold gently into the
cake batter. Pour the mixture into the prepared pan
and bake in a preheated oven, 425°F/220°C, for 7–10
minutes, or until risen and firm to the touch.

2 Transfer to a wire rack to cool completely. Wash and
dry the pan and replace the cooled cake in the pan.
Mix the coffee and brandy together and brush over
the cake.

3 To make the topping, place the cream in a bowl and
whip until very soft peaks form. Carefully fold in the
cooled chocolate. Pour the mixture over the sponge.
Let chill in the refrigerator for 4–5 hours, or until set.

4 To decorate the torte, sift unsweetened cocoa over the
top and remove carefully from the pan. Using strips of
card or waxed paper, sift bands of confectioners' sugar
over the torte to create a striped pattern. To serve, cut
into slices with a hot knife.

cookies, bars & bakes

chocolate orange cookies

ingredients

makes 30

scant ¾ cup unsalted butter, softened

generous ½ cup superfine sugar

1 egg

1 tbsp milk

2 cups all-purpose flour, plus extra for dusting

¼ cup unsweetened cocoa

frosting

1½ cups confectioners' sugar, sifted

3 tbsp orange juice

a little semisweet chocolate, broken into pieces

method

1 Line 2 cookie sheets with sheets of parchment paper. Beat together the butter and sugar until light and fluffy. Beat in the egg and milk until well combined. Sift the flour and unsweetened cocoa into the bowl and gradually mix together to form a soft dough. Use your fingers to incorporate the last of the flour and bring the dough together.

2 Roll out the dough on a lightly floured counter until ¼ inch/5 mm thick. Cut out circles using a 2-inch/ 5-cm fluted round cookie cutter. Place the circles on the prepared cookie sheets and bake in a preheated oven, 350°F/180°C, for 10–12 minutes, or until golden. Let cool on the sheet for a few minutes before transferring them to a wire rack to cool completely and become crisp.

3 To make the frosting, put the confectioners' sugar in a bowl and stir in enough orange juice to form a thin frosting that will coat the back of the spoon. Put a spoonful of frosting in the center of each cookie and let set. Place the semisweet chocolate in a heatproof bowl set over a saucepan of gently simmering water and stir until melted. Drizzle thin lines of melted chocolate over the cookies and let set before serving.

viennese fingers

ingredients

makes 16

scant ½ cup unsalted butter,
    plus extra for greasing
2 tbsp superfine sugar
½ tsp vanilla extract
scant ¼ cup self-rising flour
3½ oz/100 g semisweet chocolate,
    broken into pieces

method

1 Lightly grease 2 cookie sheets. Place the butter, sugar, and vanilla extract in a bowl and cream together until pale and fluffy. Stir in the flour, mixing evenly to a fairly stiff dough.

2 Place the mixture in a pastry bag fitted with a large star tip and pipe 16 bars, each 2½ inches/6 cm long, onto the prepared cookie sheets.

3 Bake in a preheated oven, 325°F/160°C, for 10–15 minutes, until pale golden. Cool for 2–3 minutes on the cookie sheets, then lift carefully onto a wire rack with a spatula to cool completely.

4 Place the chocolate in a small heatproof bowl set over a saucepan of gently simmering water until melted. Remove from the heat. Dip the ends of each cookie into the chocolate to coat, then place on a sheet of parchment paper and let set before serving.

variation

Pipe the mixture into star shapes using a star-shaped mold and bake. Dip the tips of the stars into a little melted chocolate.

chocolate pistachio bars

ingredients

makes 24

6 oz/175 g semisweet chocolate,
    broken into pieces
2 tbsp unsalted butter, plus extra
    for greasing
2½ cups self-rising flour, plus extra
    for dusting
1½ tsp baking powder
⅓ cup superfine sugar
½ cup cornmeal
finely grated zest of 1 lemon
2 tsp amaretto
1 egg, lightly beaten
¾ cup coarsely chopped pistachios
2 tbsp confectioners' sugar,
    for dusting

method

1 Lightly grease 2 cookie sheets with butter. Put the chocolate and butter in a heatproof bowl set over a saucepan of gently simmering water. Stir over a low heat until melted and smooth. Remove from the heat and let cool slightly.

2 Sift the flour and baking powder into a bowl and mix in the superfine sugar, cornmeal, lemon zest, amaretto, egg, and pistachios. Stir in the chocolate mixture and mix to a soft dough.

3 Lightly dust your hands with flour, divide the dough in half, and shape each piece into an 11-inch/28-cm long roll. Transfer the rolls to the prepared cookie sheets and flatten, with the palm of your hand, to about ¾ inch/2 cm thick. Bake in a preheated oven, 325°F/160°C, for about 20 minutes, or until firm to the touch.

4 Remove the cookie sheets from the oven and let the cooked pieces cool. When cool, put the cooked pieces on a cutting board and slice them diagonally into thin cookies. Return them to the cookie sheets and bake for an additional 10 minutes, or until crisp. Remove from the oven, and transfer to a wire rack to cool. Dust lightly with confectioners' sugar. Serve.

brown & white cookies

ingredients

makes 18–20

2 squares bittersweet chocolate, broken into pieces

1 cup all-purpose flour

1 tsp baking powder

1 egg

scant ¾ cup superfine sugar

scant ¼ cup corn oil, plus extra for oiling

½ tsp vanilla extract

2 tbsp confectioners' sugar

1 small package milk chocolate buttons (about 30 buttons)

1 small package white chocolate buttons (about 30 buttons)

method

1 Oil 2 large cookie sheets. Melt the bittersweet chocolate in a heatproof bowl set over a saucepan of gently simmering water. Remove from the heat and let cool. Sift the flour and baking powder together.

2 Meanwhile, in a large bowl, whip the egg, sugar, oil, and vanilla extract together. Whip in the cooled, melted chocolate until well blended, then gradually stir in the flour. Cover the bowl with plastic wrap and chill in the refrigerator for at least 3 hours.

3 Shape tablespoonfuls of the mixture into log shapes using your hands, each measuring about 2 inches/5 cm.

4 Roll the logs generously in the confectioners' sugar, then place on the prepared cookie sheets, allowing room for the cookies to spread during cooking.

5 Bake in a preheated oven, 375°F/190°C, for 15 minutes, or until firm to the touch. Remove from the oven, and place 3 chocolate buttons down the center of each, alternating the colors. Transfer to a wire rack and let cool. Serve.

chocolate chip bars

ingredients

makes 12

½ cup unsalted butter, plus extra
for greasing
generous ¼ cup superfine sugar
1 tbsp corn syrup
4 cups rolled oats
½ cup semisweet chocolate chips
⅓ cup golden raisins

method

1 Lightly grease a shallow 8-inch/20-cm square cake pan.

2 Place the butter, superfine sugar, and corn syrup in a saucepan and cook over low heat, stirring constantly, until the butter and sugar melt and the mixture is well combined.

3 Remove the pan from the heat and stir in the rolled oats until they are well coated. Add the chocolate chips and the golden raisins and mix well to combine everything together.

4 Turn the mixture into the prepared pan and press down well.

5 Bake in a preheated oven, 350°F/180°C, for 30 minutes. Cool slightly, then gently use a knife to mark into bars. When almost cooled cut into bars or squares and transfer to a wire rack to cool completely before serving.

variation

Add ⅓ cup of chopped candied cherries to the bars at the same time as the chocolate chips and raisins.

nutty chocolate drizzles

ingredients

makes 24

generous 1 cup unsalted butter, plus extra for greasing
1½ cups raw brown sugar
1 egg
1 cup all-purpose flour, sifted
1 tsp baking powder
1 tsp baking soda
1½ cups rolled oats
¼ cup bran
¼ cup wheatgerm
¾ cup mixed nuts, toasted and chopped coarsely
scant 1¾ cups semisweet chocolate chips
½ cup raisins and golden raisins
6 oz/175 g semisweet chocolate, coarsely chopped

method

1 Lightly grease two large cookie sheets. In a large bowl, cream together the butter, sugar, and egg. Add the flour, baking powder, baking soda, oats, bran, and wheatgerm and mix together until well combined. Stir in the nuts, chocoate chips, and dried fruit.

2 Put 24 rounded tablespoonfuls of the cookie mixture onto the prepared cookie sheets, allowing room for expansion during cooking. Transfer to a preheated oven, 350°F/180°C, and bake for 12 minutes, or until the cookies are golden brown.

3 Remove the cookies from the oven, then transfer to a wire rack and let cool completely. While they are cooling, put the chocolate pieces into a heatproof bowl over a pan of gently simmering water and heat until melted. Stir the chocolate, then let cool slightly. Use a spoon to drizzle the chocolate in waves over the cookies, or spoon it into a pastry bag fitted with a plain tip and and pipe zigzag lines over the cookies. Store in an airtight container in the refrigerator before serving.

white chocolate cookies

ingredients

makes 24

¼ cup butter, softened,
    plus extra for greasing
⅔ cup soft brown sugar
1 egg, beaten
generous 1¼ cups self-rising flour
pinch of salt
4½ oz/125 g white chocolate,
    coarsely chopped
generous ¼ cup Brazil nuts,
    chopped

method

1 Lightly grease 4 cookie sheets. Beat the butter and sugar together in a large bowl until light and fluffy. Gradually add the beaten egg, beating well after each addition.

2 Sift the flour and salt into the cookie batter and blend well. Stir in the white chocolate chunks and the chopped Brazil nuts.

3 Drop teaspoons of the batter onto the cookie sheets. Do not put more than 6 teaspoons of the batter onto each sheet as they will spread during cooking.

4 Bake in a preheated oven, 375°F/190°C, for 10–12 minutes, or until just golden brown. Transfer the cookies to wire racks and let cool completely before serving.

double chocolate chip cookies

ingredients

makes 24

scant 1 cup butter, softened,
    plus extra for greasing
1 cup golden superfine sugar
½ tsp vanilla extract
1 large egg
1½ cups all-purpose flour
pinch of salt
1 tsp baking soda
⅔ cup white chocolate chips
⅔ cup semisweet chocolate chips

method

1 Lightly grease 2 large cookie sheets. Place the butter, sugar, and vanilla extract in a large bowl and beat together. Gradually beat in the egg until the cookie batter is light and fluffy.

2 Sift the flour, salt, and baking soda over the cookie batter and fold in, then fold in the chocolate chips.

3 Drop 24 dessertspoonfuls of the batter onto the prepared cookie sheets, allowing room for expansion during cooking. Bake in a preheated oven, 350°F/180°C, for 10–12 minutes, or until crisp outside but still soft inside. Let cool on the cookie sheets for 2 minutes, then transfer to wire racks to cool completely before serving.

chocolate chip oaties

ingredients

makes 20

½ cup butter, softened,
plus extra for greasing
½ cup light brown sugar
1 egg
1 cup rolled oats
1 tbsp milk
1 tsp vanilla extract
scant 1 cup all-purpose flour
1 tbsp unsweetened cocoa
½ tsp baking powder
6 oz/175 g semisweet chocolate,
broken into pieces
6 oz/175 g milk chocolate,
broken into pieces

method

1 Lightly grease 2 large cookie sheets. Place the butter and sugar in a bowl and beat together until light and fluffy. Beat in the egg, then add the oats, milk, and vanilla extract. Beat together until well blended. Sift the flour, unsweetened cocoa, and baking powder into the cookie batter and stir. Stir in the chocolate pieces.

2 Place 20 dessertspoonfuls of the cookie batter onto the prepared cookie sheets, allowing room for expansion during cooking, and flatten slightly with a fork. Bake in a preheated oven, 350°F/180°C, for 15 minutes, or until slightly risen and firm to the touch. Let cool on the cookie sheets for 2 minutes, then transfer to wire racks to cool completely before serving.

apricot & chocolate chip cookies

ingredients

makes 12–14

generous ¼ cup butter, softened,
　　plus extra for greasing
2 tbsp golden granulated sugar
¼ cup light brown sugar
½ tsp vanilla extract
1 egg, beaten
generous 1 cup self-rising flour
4 oz/115 g semisweet chocolate,
　　coarsely chopped
⅔ cup no-soak dried apricots,
　　coarsely chopped

method

1 Lightly grease 2 cookie sheets. Place the butter, granulated sugar, brown sugar, and vanilla extract in a bowl and beat together. Gradually beat in the egg until light and fluffy.

2 Sift the flour over the cookie batter and fold in, then fold in the chocolate and apricots.

3 Put 12–14 tablespoonfuls of the cookie batter onto the prepared cookie sheets, allowing room for expansion during cooking. Bake in a preheated oven, 350°F/180°C, for 13–15 minutes, or until crisp outside but still soft inside. Let cool on the cookie sheets for 2 minutes, then transfer to wire racks to cool completely before serving.

chocolate & apple oaties

ingredients

makes 24

²/₃ cup apple sauce
2 tbsp apple juice
½ cup butter or margarine,
    plus extra for greasing
½ cup raw brown sugar
1 tsp baking soda
1 tsp almond extract
¼ cup boiling water
1½ cups rolled oats
2 cups all-purpose flour, unsifted
pinch of salt
⅓ cup semisweet chocolate chips

method

1 Lightly grease 2 cookie sheets. Blend the apple sauce, apple juice, butter or margarine, and sugar in a food processor until a fluffy consistency is reached.

2 In a separate bowl, mix together the baking soda, almond extract, and water, then add to the food processor and mix with the apple mixture. In another bowl, mix together the oats, flour, and salt, then gradually stir into the apple mixture and beat well. Stir in the chocolate chips.

3 Put 24 rounded tablespoonfuls of mixture onto the prepared cookie sheets, allowing room for expansion during cooking. Transfer to a preheated oven, 400°F/200°C, and bake for 15 minutes, or until the cookies are golden brown.

4 Remove the cookies from the oven, then transfer to a wire rack and let them cool completely before serving.

chocolate temptations

ingredients

makes 24

12½ oz/365 g semisweet chocolate
scant ½ cup unsalted butter,
    plus extra for greasing
1 tsp strong coffee
2 eggs
scant ¼ cup soft brown sugar
generous 1⅓ cups all-purpose flour
¼ tsp baking powder
pinch of salt
2 tsp almond extract
scant ⅔ cup Brazil nuts, chopped
scant ⅔ cup hazelnuts, chopped
1½ oz/40 g white chocolate

method

1 Lightly grease 2 large cookie sheets. Put 8 oz/225 g of the semisweet chocolate with the butter and coffee into a heatproof bowl over a pan of simmering water and heat until the chocolate is almost melted.

2 Meanwhile, beat the eggs in a bowl until fluffy. Whisk in the sugar gradually until thick. Remove the chocolate from the heat and stir until smooth, then stir it into the egg mixture until combined.

3 Sift the flour, baking powder, and salt into a bowl and stir into the chocolate mixture. Chop 3 oz/85 g of the remaining semisweet chocolate into pieces and stir into the dough. Stir in the almond extract and nuts.

4 Put 24 rounded dessertspoonfuls of the dough onto the prepared cookie sheets, allowing room for expansion during cooking. Bake in a preheated oven, 350°F/180°C, for 16 minutes. Transfer the cookies to a wire rack to cool. To decorate, melt the remaining chocolate (semisweet and white) in turn, then spoon into a pastry bag and pipe lines onto the cookies. Let set, then serve.

lebkuchen

ingredients

makes 60

3 eggs
1 cup golden superfine sugar
scant ½ cup all-purpose flour
2 tsp unsweetened cocoa
1 tsp ground cinnamon
½ tsp ground cardamom
¼ tsp ground cloves
¼ tsp ground nutmeg
1½ cups ground almonds
⅓ cup candied peel, finely chopped

to decorate

4 oz/115 g semisweet chocolate,
   melted and cooled
4 oz/115 g white chocolate,
   melted and cooled
sugar crystals

method

1 Line 3 large cookie sheets with baking parchment. Place the eggs and sugar in a small heatproof bowl and set over a pan of gently simmering water. Whisk until thick and foamy. Remove the bowl from the pan and continue to whisk for 2 minutes.

2 Sift the flour, cocoa, cinnamon, cardamom, cloves, and nutmeg over the egg mixture, add the ground almonds and chopped peel and stir. Drop teaspoonfuls of the cookie batter onto the cookie sheets, spreading them gently into smooth mounds and allowing room for expansion during cooking.

3 Bake in a preheated oven, 325°F/160°C, for 15–20 minutes, or until light brown and slightly soft to the touch. Let cool on the cookie sheets for 10 minutes, then transfer to wire racks to cool completely. Dip half the cookies in the melted semisweet chocolate and half in the white chocolate. Sprinkle with sugar crystals, let set, then serve.

checkerboard cookies

ingredients

makes 18

¾ cup butter, softened, plus extra
    for greasing
1¼ cups confectioners' sugar
1 teaspoon vanilla extract or
    grated rind of ½ orange
generous 1¾ cups all-purpose flour
1 oz/25 g semisweet chocolate
a little beaten egg white

method

1 Beat the butter and confectioners' sugar in a mixing
  bowl until light and fluffy. Beat in the vanilla extract or
  grated orange rind. Gradually beat in the flour to form
  a soft dough. Use your fingers to incorporate the last
  of the flour and bring the dough together.

2 Melt the chocolate. Divide the dough in half and beat
  the melted chocolate into one half. Keeping each
  half of the dough separate, cover, and let chill in the
  refrigerator for 30 minutes.

3 Lightly grease a large cookie sheet. Roll out each piece
  of dough to a rectangle measuring 3 x 8 inches/7.5 x
  20 cm and 1½-inches/3-cm thick. Brush one piece of
  dough with a little egg white and place the other on
  top. Cut the block of dough in half lengthwise and
  turn over one half. Brush the side of one strip with egg
  white and butt the other up to it, so that it resembles
  a checkerboard.

4 Cut the block into thin slices and place each slice flat
  on the prepared cookie sheet, allowing enough room
  for the slices to spread out a little during cooking.

5 Bake in a preheated oven, 350°F/180°C, for about
  10 minutes, or until just firm to the touch. Let cool on
  the cookie sheet for a few minutes, before transferring
  to a wire rack to cool completely before serving.

caramel chocolate shortbread

ingredients

makes 12

½ cup butter, plus extra for greasing
1¼ cups all-purpose flour
generous ¼ cup golden superfine sugar

filling and topping

¾ cup butter
generous ½ cup golden superfine sugar
3 tbsp corn syrup
14 oz/400 g canned condensed milk
7 oz/200 g semisweet chocolate, broken into pieces

method

1 Lightly grease and base-line a 9-inch/23-cm shallow square cake pan.

2 Place the butter, flour, and sugar in a food processor and process until it begins to bind together. Press the dough into the prepared pan and smooth the top. Bake in a preheated oven, 350°F/180°C, for 20–25 minutes, or until golden.

3 Meanwhile, make the filling. Place the butter, sugar, syrup, and condensed milk in a saucepan and heat gently until the sugar has melted. Bring to the boil and simmer for 6–8 minutes, stirring constantly, until the mixture becomes very thick. Pour over the shortbread base and let chill in the refrigerator until firm to the touch.

4 To make the topping, melt the chocolate and let cool, then spread over the caramel. Let chill in the refrigerator until set. Cut the shortbread into 12 pieces with a sharp knife and serve.

cappuccino squares

ingredients

makes 15

generous 1½ cups self-rising flour

1 tsp baking powder

1 tsp unsweetened cocoa,
    plus extra for dusting

1 cup butter, softened,
    plus extra for greasing

generous 1 cup golden superfine
    sugar

4 eggs, beaten

3 tbsp instant coffee powder,
    dissolved in 2 tbsp hot water

white chocolate frosting

4 oz/115 g white chocolate,
    broken into pieces

¼ cup butter, softened

3 tbsp milk

1½ cups confectioners' sugar

method

1 Lightly grease and base-line a shallow 11 x 7-inch/
    28 x 18-cm pan.

2 Sift the flour, baking powder, and cocoa into a bowl
    and add the butter, superfine sugar, eggs, and coffee.
    Beat well, by hand or with an electric whisk, until
    smooth, then spoon into the prepared pan and
    smooth the top.

3 Bake in a preheated oven, 350°F/180°C, for 35–40
    minutes, or until risen and firm to the touch, then turn
    out onto a wire rack and peel off the lining paper.
    Let cool completely.

4 To make the frosting, place the chocolate, butter, and
    milk in a bowl set over a pan of simmering water and
    stir until the chocolate has melted. Remove the bowl
    from the pan and sift in the confectioners' sugar. Beat
    until smooth, then spread over the cake. Dust the top
    of the cake with sifted cocoa, then cut into squares
    to serve.

chocolate fudge brownies

ingredients

makes 16

scant 1 cup low-fat soft cheese
½ tsp vanilla extract
1¼ cups superfine sugar
2 eggs
generous ⅓ cup butter
3 tbsp unsweetened cocoa
¾ cup self-rising flour, sifted
⅓ cup chopped pecans

fudge frosting

¼ cup butter
1 tbsp milk
⅔ cup confectioners' sugar
2 tbsp unsweetened cocoa
pecans, to decorate

method

1 Lightly grease an 8-inch/20-cm square shallow cake pan.

2 Beat together the cheese, vanilla extract, and 5 teaspoons of superfine sugar, then set aside.

3 Beat the eggs and remaining superfine sugar together until light and fluffy. Place the butter and cocoa in a small pan and heat gently, stirring until the butter melts and the mixture combines, then stir it into the egg mixture. Fold in the flour and nuts.

4 Pour half of the brownie mixture into the prepared pan and smooth the top. Carefully spread the soft cheese over it, then cover it with the remaining brownie mixture. Bake in a preheated oven, 350°F/180°C, for 40–45 minutes. Cool in the pan.

5 To make the frosting, melt the butter in the milk. Stir in the sugar and cocoa. Using a spatula, spread the frosting over the brownies and decorate with pecans. Let the frosting set, then cut into squares to serve.

mocha brownies

ingredients

makes 16

4 oz/115 g semisweet chocolate, broken into pieces

¼ cup butter, plus extra for greasing

scant 1 cup brown sugar

2 eggs

1 tbsp instant coffee powder, dissolved in 1 tbsp hot water, cooled

scant ⅔ cup all-purpose flour

½ tsp baking powder

⅓ cup coarsely chopped pecans

method

1 Lightly grease and base-line an 8-inch/20-cm square cake pan.

2 Place the chocolate and butter in a heavy-bottom pan over low heat until melted. Stir and let cool.

3 Place the sugar and eggs in a large bowl and cream together until light and fluffy. Fold in the chocolate mixture and cooled coffee and mix thoroughly. Sift in the flour and baking powder and lightly fold into the mixture, then carefully fold in the pecans.

4 Pour the batter into the prepared pan and bake in a preheated oven, 350°F/180°C, for 25–30 minutes, or until firm to the touch and a skewer inserted into the center comes out clean.

5 Let cool in the pan for a few minutes, then run a knife round the edge of the cake to loosen it. Turn the cake out onto a wire rack and peel off the lining paper. Let cool completely. When cold, cut into squares and serve.

refrigerator cake

ingredients

makes 12

⅓ cup raisins

2 tbsp brandy

4 oz/115 g semisweet chocolate, broken into pieces

4 oz/115 g milk chocolate, broken into pieces

¼ cup butter, plus extra for greasing

2 tbsp corn syrup

6 oz/175 g graham crackers, coarsely broken

½ cup slivered almonds, lightly toasted

¼ cup candied cherries, chopped

topping

3½ oz/100 g semisweet chocolate, broken into pieces

scant 2 tbsp butter

method

1 Lightly grease and base-line a 7-inch/18-cm shallow square pan.

2 Place the raisins and brandy in a bowl and let soak for 30 minutes. Put the chocolate, butter, and syrup in a pan and heat gently until melted.

3 Stir in the graham crackers, almonds, cherries, raisins, and brandy. Turn into the prepared pan and let cool. Cover and let chill in the refrigerator for 1 hour.

4 To make the topping, place the chocolate and butter in a small heatproof bowl and melt over a pan of gently simmering water. Stir and pour the chocolate mixture over the cookie base. Let chill in the refrigerator for 8 hours, or overnight. Cut into bars or squares to serve.

chocolates & petits fours

chocolate almond petits fours

ingredients
makes 16

½ cup ground almonds
⅓ cup granulated sugar
5 tsp unsweetened cocoa
1 egg white
8 blanched almonds, halved
2 oz/55 g semisweet chocolate,
    broken into pieces

method

1 Line a cookie sheet with parchment paper.

2 Put the ground almonds, sugar, and unsweetened cocoa in a bowl and mix together well. Add the egg white and mix to form a firm mixture.

3 Fill a pastry bag, fitted with a small plain tip, with the mixture and pipe 2-inch/5-cm lengths, spaced well apart, onto the prepared cookie sheet. Place an almond half on top of each.

4 Bake in a preheated oven, 375°F/190°C, for about 5 minutes, or until firm to the touch. Transfer to a wire rack and let cool.

5 When the petits fours have cooled, melt the chocolate in a heatproof bowl set over a saucepan of gently simmering water. Dip each end of the petits fours into the melted chocolate, then let stand on the wire rack to set completely.

chocolate creams

ingredients

makes 30

7 oz/200 g semisweet chocolate,
    broken into pieces
2 tbsp light cream
2 cups confectioners' sugar
drinking chocolate powder,
    for dusting

method

1 Line a cookie sheet with parchment paper.

2 Melt 2 oz/55 g of the chocolate in a large heatproof bowl set over a saucepan of gently simmering water. Stir in the cream and remove the bowl from the heat.

3 Sift the confectioners' sugar into the melted chocolate then, using a fork, mix well together. Knead to form a firm, smooth, pliable mixture.

4 Lightly dust a counter with drinking chocolate powder, turn out the mixture, and roll out to ¼-inch/5-mm thickness, then cut into circles, using a 1-inch/2.5-cm plain round cutter.

5 Transfer the rounds to the prepared cookie sheet and let stand for about 12 hours, or overnight, until set and dry.

6 Melt the remaining chocolate in a heatproof bowl set over a saucepan of gently simmering water. Using two forks, carefully dip each chocolate cream into the melted chocolate. Lift them out quickly, letting any excess chocolate drain against the side of the bowl, and place on the prepared cookie sheet. Let set.

ginger chocolate fudge

ingredients

makes 50

6 pieces preserved ginger,
plus extra for decorating
(optional)
1¼ cups milk
5½ oz/150 g bittersweet chocolate,
broken into pieces
½ cup unsalted butter, plus extra
for greasing
2⅓ cups granulated sugar

method

1 Lightly grease a 7-inch/18-cm shallow square pan
or an 8 x 6-inch/20 x 15-cm shallow pan.

2 Dry the syrup off the pieces of preserved ginger on
paper towels, then chop finely.

3 Pour the milk into a large, heavy-bottom saucepan
and add the chocolate, butter, and sugar. Heat gently,
stirring all the time, until the chocolate and butter
have melted and the sugar has dissolved.

4 Bring to a boil and then boil for about 10–15 minutes,
stirring occasionally, until a little of the mixture, when
dropped into a small bowl of cold water, forms a soft
ball when rolled between your fingers.

5 Remove the saucepan from the heat and stir in the
chopped ginger. Let cool for 5 minutes, then beat the
mixture vigorously with a wooden spoon until thick,
creamy, and grainy.

6 Immediately pour the mixture into the prepared pan,
let cool, then mark into small squares. Leave the fudge
until cooled and set, then cut into squares with a
sharp knife. Decorate with pieces of preserved ginger,
if wished.

easy chocolate fudge

ingredients

makes 25

1 lb 2 oz/500 g semisweet
chocolate

⅓ cup unsalted butter, cut into
even-size pieces, plus extra
for greasing

14 oz/400 g canned sweetened
condensed milk

½ tsp vanilla extract

method

1 Lightly grease an 8-inch/20-cm square cake pan with butter.

2 Break the chocolate into small pieces and place in a large, heavy-bottom pan with the butter and condensed milk.

3 Heat gently, stirring constantly, until the chocolate and butter melt and the mixture is smooth. Do not let boil. Remove from the heat. Beat in the vanilla extract, then beat the mixture for a few minutes until thickened. Pour the mixture into the prepared pan and level the top.

4 Let the mixture chill in the refrigerator for 1 hour, or until firm to the touch. Tip the fudge out onto a cutting board and cut into squares to serve.

pecan mocha fudge

ingredients

makes 80

1¼ cups milk

generous 5 cups golden granulated sugar

1 generous cup butter, plus extra for greasing

2 tbsp instant coffee granules

2 tbsp unsweetened cocoa

2 tbsp corn syrup

14 oz/400 g canned condensed milk

½ cup shelled pecans, chopped

method

1 Lightly grease a 12 x 9-inch/30 x 23-cm jelly roll pan.

2 Place the milk, sugar, and butter in a large pan. Stir over gentle heat until the sugar has dissolved. Stir in the coffee granules, cocoa, syrup, and condensed milk.

3 Bring to a boil and boil steadily, whisking constantly, for 10 minutes, or until a temperature of 241°F/116°C has been reached on a sugar thermometer, or a small amount of the mixture forms a soft ball when dropped into cold water.

4 Let cool for 5 minutes, then beat vigorously with a wooden spoon until the mixture starts to thicken. Stir in the nuts. Continue beating until the mixture takes on a fudge-like consistency. Quickly pour into the prepared pan and let stand in a cool place to set. Cut the fudge into squares to serve.

white chocolate truffles

ingredients

makes 12

2 tbsp unsalted butter
scant ⅓ cup heavy cream
8 oz/225 g good-quality Swiss
　　white chocolate
1 tbsp orange-flavored liqueur
　　(optional)

to finish

3½ oz/100 g white chocolate

method

1 Line a jelly roll pan with a sheet of baking parchment.

2 Place the butter and cream in a small pan and bring slowly to a boil, stirring constantly. Boil the mixture for 1 minute, then remove the pan from the heat.

3 Break the chocolate into pieces and add to the cream. Stir until melted, then beat in the orange-flavored liqueur, if using. Pour into the prepared pan and let chill in the refrigerator for about 2 hours, or until firm to the touch.

4 Break off pieces of the truffle mixture and roll them into balls. Let chill in the refrigerator for an additional 30 minutes before finishing the truffles.

5 To finish, melt the white chocolate in a bowl set over a pan of gently simmering water. Dip the balls in the chocolate, allowing the excess to drip back into the bowl. Place on nonstick parchment, swirl the chocolate with the tines of a fork, and let harden.

variation

Use 3½ oz/100 g semisweet or milk chocolate instead of the white chocolate to finish the truffles.

irish cream truffles

ingredients

makes 24

generous ⅔ cup heavy cream
8 oz/225 g semisweet chocolate,
    broken into pieces
2 tbsp butter
3 tbsp Irish cream liqueur

to finish

4 oz/115 g white chocolate,
    broken into pieces
4 oz/115 g semisweet chocolate,
    broken into pieces

method

1 Heat the cream in a pan over low heat but do not let
boil. Remove from the heat and stir in the chocolate
and butter. Let stand for 2 minutes, then stir until
smooth. Stir in the liqueur. Pour the mixture into a
bowl and let cool. Cover and let chill in the refrigerator
for 8 hours, or overnight, or until firm to the touch.

2 Line a cookie sheet with nonstick parchment paper.
Take 24 teaspoonfuls of the chilled chocolate mixture
and roll into small balls. Place the balls on the prepared
cookie sheet and let chill in the refrigerator for 2–4
hours, or until firm to the touch.

3 Melt the white chocolate pieces and let cool slightly.
Coat half the truffles by spearing on thin skewers or
toothpicks and dipping into the white chocolate.
Transfer to a sheet of nonstick parchment paper to
set. Melt the semisweet chocolate and let cool slightly,
then use to coat the remaining truffles in the same
way. Store the truffles in the refrigerator in an airtight
container, separated by layers of waxed paper, for up
to one week.

rum truffles

ingredients

makes 12

4½ oz/125 g semisweet
    chocolate
small piece of butter
2 tbsp rum
½ cup shredded coconut
scant 1 cup cake crumbs
generous ½ cup confectioners'
    sugar
2 tbsp unsweetened cocoa

method

1 Line a cookie sheet with baking parchment. Break the chocolate into pieces and place in a bowl with the butter. Set the bowl over a pan of gently simmering water and stir until melted and combined.

2 Remove from the heat and beat in the rum. Stir in the shredded coconut, cake crumbs, and two-thirds of the confectioners' sugar. Beat until combined. Add a little extra rum if the mixture is stiff.

3 Roll the mixture into small balls and place them on the prepared cookie sheet. Chill in the refrigerator until firm to the touch.

4 Sift the remaining confectioners' sugar onto a large plate. Sift the cocoa onto another plate. Roll half of the truffles in the confectioners' sugar until thoroughly coated and roll the remaining rum truffles in the cocoa.

5 Place the truffles in paper candy cases or arrange on a plate and let chill in the refrigerator.

chocolate orange collettes

ingredients

makes 20

10 oz/280 g semisweet chocolate,
    broken into pieces
½ tsp corn oil
⅔ cup heavy cream
finely grated rind of ½ orange
1 tbsp Cointreau

to decorate

chopped nuts
fine strips of orange rind

method

1 Melt 5½ oz/150 g of the chocolate with the oil and stir until mixed. Spread evenly over the inside of 20 double petit four cases, taking care to keep a good thickness round the edge. Let chill in the refrigerator for 1 hour, or until set, then apply a second coat of chocolate, remelting if necessary. Let chill in the refrigerator for 1 hour, or until completely set.

2 Place the cream and grated orange rind in a pan and heat until almost boiling. Remove from the heat, add the remaining chocolate pieces and stir until smooth. Return to the heat and stir until the mixture starts to bubble. Remove from the heat and stir in the Cointreau. Let cool. Peel the paper cases off the chocolate cups.

3 Beat the chocolate cream until thick, then spoon into a large pastry bag fitted with a fluted tip. Pipe the chocolate cream into the chocolate cases. Decorate some of the chocolate collettes with chopped nuts and some with a few strips of orange rind. Cover and keep in the refrigerator. Use within 2–3 days.

chocolate liqueurs

ingredients

makes 20

3½ oz/100 g semisweet chocolate
5 candied cherries, halved
10 hazelnuts or macadamia nuts
⅔ cup heavy cream
2 tbsp confectioners' sugar
4 tbsp liqueur of your choice

to finish

1¾ oz/50 g semisweet
    chocolate, melted
a little white chocolate, melted, or
    white chocolate curls, or extra
    nuts and cherries

method

1 Line a cookie sheet with a sheet of baking parchment. Break the semisweet chocolate into pieces, place in a bowl and set over a pan of hot water. Stir until melted. Spoon the chocolate into 20 double-layer paper candy cases, spreading up the sides with a small spoon or brush. Place upside down on the cookie sheet and let set.

2 Carefully peel away the paper cases. Place a cherry or nut in the bottom of each cup.

3 To make the filling, place the heavy cream in a mixing bowl and sift the confectioners' sugar on top. Whip the cream until it is just holding its shape, then whip in the liqueur to flavor it.

4 Place the cream in a pastry bag fitted with a ½-inch/ 1-cm plain tip and pipe a little into each chocolate case. Let chill in the refrigerator for 20 minutes.

5 To finish, spoon the semisweet chocolate over the cream to cover it and pipe the melted white chocolate on top, swirling it into the semisweet chocolate with a toothpick. Let harden. Alternatively, cover the cream with the melted semisweet chocolate and decorate with white chocolate curls before setting. If you prefer, place a small piece of nut or cherry on top of the cream, then cover with semisweet chocolate.

chocolate mascarpone cups

ingredients

makes 20

3½ oz/100 g semisweet
   chocolate

filling

3½ oz/100 g milk or semisweet
   chocolate
1 cup mascarpone cheese
¼ tsp vanilla extract
unsweetened cocoa, for dusting

method

1 Line a cookie sheet with a sheet of baking parchment.
   Break the semisweet chocolate into pieces, place in a
   bowl and set over a pan of hot water. Stir until melted.
   Spoon the chocolate into 20 paper candy cases,
   spreading up the sides with a small spoon or brush.
   Place the chocolate cups upside down on the cookie
   sheet and let set. When set, carefully peel away the
   paper cases.

2 To make the filling, melt the chocolate. Place the
   mascarpone cheese in a bowl and beat in the vanilla
   extract and melted chocolate until well combined.
   Let the mixture chill in the refrigerator, beating
   occasionally, or until firm enough to pipe.

3 Place the mascarpone filling in a pastry bag fitted with
   a star tip and pipe the mixture into the cups. Decorate
   with a dusting of cocoa.

mini chocolate cones

ingredients

makes 10

2¾ oz/75 g semisweet chocolate
generous ⅓ cup heavy cream
1 tbsp confectioners' sugar
1 tbsp crème de menthe

method

1 Cut 10 x 3-inch/7.5-cm circles of parchment paper. Shape each circle into a cone shape and secure with a piece of sticky tape.

2 Break the chocolate into pieces, place in a heatproof bowl, and set over a pan of hot water. Stir until the chocolate has melted. Using a small pastry brush or clean artist's brush, brush the inside of each cone with the melted chocolate.

3 Brush a second layer of chocolate on the inside of the cones and let chill in the refrigerator for 2 hours, or until set. Carefully peel away the paper.

4 Place the cream, confectioners' sugar, and crème de menthe in a large bowl and whip until just holding its shape. Place in a pastry bag fitted with a star tip and pipe the mixture into the chocolate cones. Let chill in the refrigerator for 1–2 hours.

brazil nut brittle

ingredients

makes 20

oil, for brushing

12 oz/350 g semisweet chocolate, broken into pieces

scant ¾ cup shelled Brazil nuts, chopped

6 oz/175 g white chocolate, coarsely chopped

6 oz/175 g fudge, coarsely chopped

method

1 Brush the bottom of an 8-inch/20-cm square cake pan with oil and line with parchment paper. Melt half the semisweet chocolate and spread in the prepared pan.

2 Sprinkle with the chopped Brazil nuts, white chocolate, and fudge. Melt the remaining semisweet chocolate pieces and pour over the top.

3 Let the brittle set, then break up into jagged pieces using the tip of a strong knife.

nutty chocolate clusters

ingredients

makes 30

6 oz/175 g white chocolate

3½ oz/100 g graham crackers

⅔ cup chopped macadamia nuts or brazil nuts

scant 3 tbsp preserved ginger, chopped (optional)

6 oz/175 g semisweet chocolate

method

1 Line a cookie sheet with a sheet of baking parchment. Break the white chocolate into small pieces and melt in a large mixing bowl set over a pan of gently simmering water.

2 Break the graham crackers into small pieces. Stir the crackers into the melted chocolate with the chopped nuts and preserved ginger, if using.

3 Place 30 teaspoons of the chocolate cluster mixture onto the prepared cookie sheet. Let chill in the refrigerator until set, then carefully remove from the baking parchment.

4 Melt the semisweet chocolate and let cool slightly. Dip the clusters into the chocolate, letting the excess drip back into the bowl. Return to the cookie sheet and let chill until set.

apricot & almond clusters

ingredients

makes 24–28

4 oz/115 g semisweet chocolate,
broken into pieces

2 tbsp honey

²/₃ cup no-soak dried apricots,
chopped

scant ¹/₂ cup blanched almonds,
chopped

method

1 Place the chocolate and honey in a bowl and set over
a pan of gently simmering water until the chocolate
has melted. Stir in the apricots and almonds.

2 Drop teaspoonfuls of the mixture into petit four cases.
Let set for 2–4 hours, or until firm to the touch.

chocolate cherries

ingredients

makes 24

12 candied cherries
2 tbsp rum or brandy
9 oz/250 g marzipan
5½ oz/125 g semisweet
    chocolate
milk, semisweet, or white
    chocolate, to decorate

method

1 Cut the candied cherries in half and place in a small
   bowl. Add the rum or brandy and stir to coat. Let the
   cherries soak for at least 1 hour, stirring occasionally.

2 Line a cookie sheet with a sheet of baking parchment.
   Divide the marzipan into 24 pieces and roll each piece
   into a ball. Press half a cherry into the top of each
   marzipan ball.

3 Break the chocolate into pieces, place in a bowl, and
   set over a pan of hot water. Stir until melted. Dip each
   candy into the melted chocolate using a toothpick,
   allowing the excess to drip back into the bowl. Place
   the coated cherries on the baking parchment and let
   chill in the refrigerator until set.

4 Melt a little extra chocolate and drizzle it over the top
   of the coated cherries. Let set.

ladies' kisses

ingredients

makes 20

scant ¾ cup unsalted butter
generous ½ cup superfine sugar
1 egg yolk
generous 1 cup ground almonds
generous 1 cup all-purpose flour
2 oz/55 g semisweet chocolate,
    broken into pieces
2 tbsp confectioners' sugar
2 tbsp unsweetened cocoa

method

1 Beat the butter and sugar together in a bowl until pale and fluffy. Beat in the egg yolk, then beat in the almonds and flour. Continue beating until well mixed. Shape the dough into a ball, wrap in plastic wrap, and let chill in the refrigerator for 1½–2 hours.

2 Line three cookie sheets with parchment paper. Unwrap the dough, break off walnut-size pieces, and roll them into balls between the palms of your hands. Place the dough balls on the prepared sheets, allowing room for expansion during cooking. Bake in a preheated oven, 325°F/160°C, for 20–25 minutes, or until golden brown. Carefully transfer the cookies, still on the parchment paper, to wire racks to cool.

3 Place the semisweet chocolate in a small heatproof bowl and set over a pan of barely simmering water, stirring constantly, until melted. Remove from the heat.

4 Remove the cookies from the parchment paper and spread the melted chocolate over the bases. Sandwich together in pairs and return to the wire racks to cool completely. Dust with the sugar and cocoa and serve.

variation

Use 1 cup of ground hazelnuts instead of the ground almonds.

mini florentines

ingredients

makes 40

⅓ cup butter, plus extra for greasing
scant ⅓ cup superfine sugar
2 tbsp golden raisins
2 tbsp chopped candied cherries
2 tbsp chopped candied ginger
generous 3 tbsp sunflower seeds
¼ cup slivered almonds
2 tbsp heavy cream
6 oz/175 g semisweet chocolate

method

1 Grease and flour 2 cookie sheets or line them with baking parchment.

2 Gently heat the butter in a small pan until melted. Add the sugar, stir until dissolved, then bring the mixture to a boil. Remove from the heat and stir in the golden raisins, cherries, ginger, sunflower seeds, and almonds. Mix well, then beat in the cream.

3 Place small teaspoons of the fruit and nut mixture onto the prepared cookie sheets, allowing plenty of space for the mixture to spread. Bake in a preheated oven, at 350°F/180°C, for 10–12 minutes, or until light golden in color. Remove from the oven and, while still hot, use a circular cookie cutter to pull in the edges to form perfect circles. Let cool and go crisp before removing from the cookie sheets.

4 Break the chocolate into pieces, place in a bowl over a pan of hot water, and stir until melted. Spread most of the chocolate onto a sheet of baking parchment. When nearly set, place the cookies flat-side down on the chocolate and let harden completely.

5 Cut around the florentines and remove from the baking parchment. Spread a little more chocolate on the coated side of the florentines and use a fork to mark waves in the chocolate. Let set and keep cool.

chocolate biscotti

ingredients

makes 16

1 egg
1/2 cup superfine sugar
1 tsp vanilla extract
scant 1 cup all-purpose flour
1/2 tsp baking powder
1 tsp ground cinnamon
1 3/4 oz/50 g semisweet chocolate,
  coarsely chopped
1/2 cup toasted slivered almonds
1/3 cup pine nuts

method

1 Lightly grease a large cookie sheet. Whisk the egg, sugar, and vanilla extract in a mixing bowl with an electric mixer until thick and pale—ribbons of mixture should trail from the whisk as you lift it.

2 Sift the flour, baking powder, and cinnamon into a separate bowl, then sift into the egg mixture and fold in gently. Stir in the coarsely chopped semisweet chocolate, toasted slivered almonds, and pine nuts.

3 Turn out onto a lightly floured counter and shape into a flat log, 9-inches/23-cm long and 3/4-inch/1.5-cm wide. Transfer to the prepared cookie sheet.

4 Bake in a preheated oven, 350°F/180°C, for 20–25 minutes, or until golden. Remove the cookie log from the oven and let cool for 5 minutes, or until firm to the touch.

5 Transfer the log to a cutting board. Using a serrated bread knife, cut the log on the diagonal into slices about 1/2 inch/1 cm thick and arrange them on the cookie sheet. Cook for 10–15 minutes, turning halfway through the cooking time.

6 Let cool for about 5 minutes, then transfer to a wire rack to cool completely.

index